This copy of
THE PRIZE PONY
by Josephine Pullein-Thompson
belongs to

Other Sparrow Books by Josephine Pullein-Thompson

The No-Good Pony

Josephine Pullein-Thompson

The Prize Pony

For Penelope Fitzgerald and her daughter, who wrote a story and won a pony . . .

A Sparrow Book
Published by Arrow Books Limited
17–21 Conway Street, London W1P 6JD

An imprint of the Hutchinson Publishing Group

London Melbourne Sydney Auckland
Johannesburg and agencies
throughout the world

First published 1982

Set in Linoterm Baskerville
by Book Economy Services, Burgess Hill, Sussex

Made and printed in Great Britain
by the Anchor Press Ltd
Tiptree, Essex

ISBN 09 928020 5

Contents

1	A dream come true	7
2	Easter parade	19
3	Too good for the Petersons	30
4	Don't tell Mum	39
5	Riding's no fun	50
6	I'm just not good enough	63
7	The hunter trials	78
8	The money belongs to Debbie	96

1

A dream come true

Debbie Peterson sat down on the window seat in the kitchen at number seven Long View Road and re-read the elegantly typewritten letter. She felt stunned; the words were still unbelievable even at the second reading. She looked across the table at her mother eating and drinking absentmindedly as she read the morning paper, then down at Tess, her younger sister, kneeling on the floor as she brushed Wolfgang, the family dog. Her father and Rachel were still upstairs, it was the first Saturday of the Easter holidays, so no one was rushing off to school or work.

Debbie read her letter again, very carefully, to make sure there was no mistake, then she said, 'Mum, read this. I *think* it says I've won first prize.'

'What's that, love?' asked Mrs Peterson taking the letter.

'First prize for what?' asked Tess, releasing Wolfgang and coming over to look.

'The story I wrote. I posted it off weeks and weeks ago.'

'You've won all right, darling,' said Mrs Peterson. 'But, oh dear, what on earth are *we* going to do with a *pony*?'

'You mean she's won that story competition, she's really won a pony?' Tess grabbed the letter and then gave a whoop of joy. 'She has! A pony in the family at last.' Waving the letter, she rushed out of the room.

'Rae, Dad, Deb's won a pony,' they could hear her shouting as she thundered upstairs.

Mrs Peterson made herself a second cup of coffee. Debbie stared out of the window; she didn't see their small garden, or the fields and woods beyond, that were just losing the grey drabness of winter and turning green. She stared, but saw nothing as she thought, *of course* it's no use. We've nowhere to keep a pony and with Dad only able to work part-time we can't afford hay. I'll have to write back and say we haven't a field or stable. I suppose they'll give it to the person who was second. She struggled to control the tears that were pricking behind her eyes.

They could hear Tess reading the contents of the letter outside the bathroom door. She was shouting to be heard above the running taps.

Mrs Peterson sat down at the table, took a drink of her coffee and sighed. 'Oh dear,' she said again. 'You know, Deb, money only becomes important when you have children. If you're on your own being short of cash doesn't matter, you live on baked beans for a bit or go without new clothes. But once you've got children you long to give them all the things they want and need; it hurts terribly when you simply can't afford to. And then with three of you, we have to try to be fair.'

'It's all right,' lied Debbie. 'I knew I couldn't really have a pony; I just wanted to see if my story was good enough to win.'

'I'll talk it over with Dad, but things have been so difficult since his accident, I just don't see how we could manage it.'

Tess came thundering down the stairs. 'Dad's reading the letter for himself,' she said. 'He didn't believe it at first, but now he thinks it's absolutely terrific. What's the matter?' she asked, looking from her mother to Debbie. 'Why aren't you pleased?'

'I just don't see how we can possibly afford to keep a pony,' answered Mrs Peterson.

'Oh, Mummy, we *must* have it,' Tess told her. 'Debbie's won it, she's actually won a pony. You know we've always wanted one and anyway, you can't refuse a prize. We'll *make* money, baby-sitting and things; I'll help.'

'But they cost such a lot,' explained Mrs Peterson sadly. 'There's grazing, hay and oats to start with. Then add shoes and vets' bills, saddlery and riding clothes – it comes to a fortune. I've talked to the other mothers at school, and unless you have your own paddock or you're a farmer the costs are terrifying. And you've *got* to find the money; you can't let ponies starve, or go without vets and shoes. We've gone through some hard times in the last two years and now, just when things are beginning to get a bit easier. . . .' her voice shook.

'It's all right,' Debbie told her quickly, 'I understand and I don't mind, *really*.'

Tess looked horrified. 'But you can't mean you're going to say no, Mummy. We'll never have a chance like this again. You don't seem to realize that Deb has actually *won* a pony, we haven't got to buy one; it's ours.'

'Don't go on at me, darling,' said Mrs Peterson. 'I do realize what a disappointment it is, especially for Deb, but I'm the one who does the shopping, worries about the heating bills and tries to find the money for *your* shoes, and that's difficult enough; I just can't face another mouth to feed.'

Tess looked across at her sister, bent, wooden-faced, over the toaster. 'Oh, well, Deb doesn't seem to care much, so I suppose it doesn't matter,' she said angrily.

Debbie didn't try to explain, she couldn't trust herself to speak, but she was glad to hear her father's slow step on the stairs. He came limping into the room. 'Well *done*, Deb,' he said, brandishing the letter. 'The first Peterson to win a prize for writing. Many congratulations, love,' he added, kissing her. 'I hope you've kept a copy of the story, I'd like to read it.

'Now, I see the "presentation ceremony" is next Friday and you're invited to bring your immediate family, which means I must ask for the day off. And then we've got to find somewhere to keep this pony.'

'Oh, Mike, don't,' said Mrs Peterson. 'We can't possibly afford it. We *can't* put ourselves on the breadline again by taking on a pony.'

'But we don't have to support it,' answered Mr Peterson cheerfully. 'You mean that you haven't read page two of this communication? "A saddle, bridle, headcollar and complete grooming kit, together with veterinary insurance and a sufficient sum to provide for the pony's keep and shoeing for one year, are part of the prize",' he read out.

Tess gave a cheer. 'Oh, great – terrific! You can have him after all, Deb.' She began to dance round the kitchen.

Mrs Peterson took the letter and studied the second page carefully. 'You're right,' she agreed, looking more cheerful, 'but at the end of the year, when the girls have all fallen in love with him, what then?'

'With any luck I'll be a hundred per cent recovered and back in a full-time job. You have to take a chance sometimes.'

'Yes, Dad's right,' shouted Tess, still dancing round the kitchen and encouraging Wolfgang to bark excitedly, 'you've got to take risks in life.'

Then Rachel appeared. 'Did someone say that Deb had won a pony?' she asked sleepily.

'Yes, and a year's keep and tack,' shouted Tess.

'And we're all invited to the presentation, it's being held at the Southgate Equestrian School at Richmond, near London,' said Mrs Peterson, who was still reading the second page of the letter. 'In the covered school, with the directors of Stir-a-Brek breakfast foods and the press present. Next Friday. Oh Lord, what *am* I going to wear?'

Debbie handed out toast. She felt strangely numb. She had won and then lost the pony too quickly to become used to either state. It was no use getting excited, probably something else would go wrong, she thought sadly.

'Isn't it fantastic, Rae, everyone at school's going to be green with envy, half my form sent stories in. And what about Melanie Jones? She won't be able to be so snobby when we've got a pony too. Oh, I do hope they give you a really lovely one, Deb, ten times better than Copper.'

'Well, don't go boasting to all your friends till we see what sort of pony it is,' Rachel told Tess. 'It may turn out to be a Shetland or something and then we'll look pretty silly.'

'No, they say as soon as Debbie lets them know her age, weight, height and riding experience, "three or four ponies will be selected from which she will make her final choice on the day, and she will be assisted in making her choice by the well-known showjumping rider Brian Bateman".'

'Brian Bateman,' shrieked Tess. 'It gets more and more terrific. Oh, Deb, you are lucky. Do you think he'll give me his autograph? And one for my friend, Karen? He's her favourite showjumper.'

Debbie made more toast and looked at her sisters. Tess, she thought, was really pleased that she had won, but Rachel wasn't. Because she was the eldest, Rae always thought she should be best at everything. She was the most brainy, she did the best at school and she was the prettiest, thought Debbie; that ought to be enough. They all had the same smooth black hair, bright blue eyes and rather square white teeth, which showed when they smiled, so people always knew at once that they were sisters. But Rae's hair was long and glamorous and Mummy said she moved beautifully and could be a model, only she didn't recommend it, as it was such a hard life. Tess's hair was short. She looked cheeky and crashed through life noisily, but everyone loved her and she had dozens of friends. It was difficult being the middle one, thought Debbie. She wasn't the beautiful grown-up one like Rae nor the jolly little baby like Tess. She was just dull old Deb in the middle. Even her hair was middling. Sometimes she grew it to look like Rae and sometimes she had it all cut off to look like Tess; now it was in between and a bit of a disaster. Rae shouldn't grudge her a prize for writing, she thought, except that, of course, having a pony was a really big thing. It would change all their lives. She tried to imagine it. If the pony ever actually arrived she would share it with Tess and Rae, she decided. They would have equal turns.

'Can you still fit in Rachel's jodhs, Deb?' asked her mother. 'And what about boots and a crash cap? With all these directors and the press there you must look reasonably tidy.'

Before their father had had the car accident, the Petersons had ridden once a week at a local riding school, but that was two years ago so they had all grown and the riding clothes had been passed down. Debbie was two years older than Tess so her jodhs now fitted Tess perfectly, but, with only a year between them, Rachel's had become very tight on Debbie.

'I think I can still squeeze into them,' she said.

'We'd better have a trying-on session this morning,' decided her mother. 'It would be awful if you couldn't mount or they split.'

'Now, what about somewhere to keep the pony?' asked Mr Peterson. 'I draw the line at having him in the garage, so you'd better start looking at once, Deb. What about asking Mrs Jones if you can keep him with Melanie's pony?'

'Dad! You know we can't stand Melanie or Mrs Jones,' protested Rachel indignantly.

'I thought that was because, being pony-less, we weren't in the same league? Now everything will change, you'll probably become bosom friends.'

'Not with stuck-up Melanie,' shrieked Tess.

'Well, what about Mrs Yaxley then?' suggested Mr Peterson. 'She's always glad to give advice.'

'The bossiest person in Cutters' Green,' objected Tess.

'She knows everyone in the pony club,' said Debbie, 'I think we should ask her first.'

'Yes, and at least her advice is sound; she was a farmer's daughter and brought up with horses. Mrs Jones puts on such airs, but she doesn't really know a thing,' added Mrs Peterson.

'Right then, when we've written to Stir-a-Brek, Deb goes to see Mrs Yaxley.'

'I'll come with you, Deb,' offered Tess. 'We might see Ricky,' she giggled self-consciously.

'I might come along too,' said Rachel in a disinterested voice, and then glared at Tess who giggled again.

'I don't see why you have to pretend you don't want to see him,' protested Tess. 'Everyone agrees that he's the best-looking boy for miles around. All my form are crazy about him, they think he ought to be a film star. They're all mad with envy that I live so near him.'

'I hope you don't go round giving the impression that we live in a posh cottage on Cutters' Green,' said Rachel.

'No, of course I don't. Everyone knows that Long

View Road is on the estate, but I live nearer to him than any of the others.'

'What I've never been able to make out is how a hideous couple like Clive and Joan Yaxley managed to produce Richard,' said Mr Peterson pausing between mouthfuls of cornflakes. 'Do you think the babies were mixed up in hospital, and that somewhere there's a disconsolate mother looking at a son with Clive Yaxley's nose and wondering where it came from?'

'Perhaps really they adopted him as well as Sam,' suggested Debbie.

'No, I'm sure it's true that they didn't want Ricky to grow up an only, and adopted Sam when they found they couldn't have another child,' said Mrs Peterson. 'Joan told me herself.'

'I expect they regret it now that Sam's turned out to be a bit of a disaster,' observed Rachel.

'I don't think Sam's a disaster exactly,' argued her mother. 'It's just that Ricky is good-looking and charming and such a good rider that Sam's put in the shade.'

'Oh, Mummy, he's pathetic. He never speaks,' objected Rachel. 'And he's hideous, red hair and freckles – ugh!'

'Every one in my form thinks he's weird,' announced Tess firmly. 'And Melanie Jones thinks he's weird, too, and she ought to know as she's Ricky's girlfriend.'

Debbie didn't think Sam was that bad and anyway she felt sorry for him; he seemed to spend his life watching Ricky win prizes and hearing him admired. She wondered what he felt like inside, whether he was jealous of his adopted brother.

They took the Stir-a-Brek letter to show Mrs Yaxley.

'She'll never believe us otherwise,' Debbie said, stuffing it in her anorak pocket, 'and it'll take hours of explaining.'

'It's so *exciting*,' said Tess, cantering round her sisters as they walked sedately down Long View Road between the neat houses, with their painted gates and tidy gardens full of tulips and forget-me-nots. 'What do you think the pony will be like? An exquisite dapple grey, a rich conker-like bay? If Brian Bateman's choosing him he'll probably be a showjumper, Deb, have you thought of that?'

'I wouldn't expect too much. By the time Stir-a-Brek have paid for the tack and the year's keep and all the rest of it they're not going to have much to spend on the actual pony,' Rachel told her.

'I think he'll be really gorgeous,' Tess argued, 'after all, they're having the newspapers there to photograph him and everything. I think he'll be the most beautiful pony in the world and everyone we know will be mad with envy. What are you going to call him, Deb? Oh, do cheer up, you don't seem a bit excited or pleased or anything.'

'I am, really,' answered Debbie, who was rehearsing her opening words to Mrs Yaxley. 'It's just that there's such a lot to arrange and sort out before it starts being fun.'

'Dad's right when he says that Cutters' Green isn't real any more,' remarked Rachel. She looked critically at the trim turf encircled by the picturesque and carefully restored cottages and the blossom of the wild cherry trees, dazzlingly white in the spring sunshine. 'There ought to be a few cows about, a farmer on a tractor and some mud.'

'I wish there was still a blacksmith at the old forge,' said Debbie, wondering what to do about getting her pony shod.

Jasmine cottage, the Yaxleys' house, was pink painted and quite large, three cottages having been made into one. The Petersons went in through the white five-barred gate at the side which led into a little yard with two modern loose boxes, a tack room, garage and hay store.

Mrs Yaxley, wearing trousers and an old sweater, her grey hair straight and cut squarely round her uncared-for face, was sweeping the concrete with a gigantic broom. Debbie went up to her and spoke her prepared words. 'Oh, Mrs Yaxley, something rather exciting has happened, I've won a pony.' Hastily she forestalled questions by handing over the letter.

Mrs Yaxley read it slowly and carefully, then she said, 'Oh, Debbie, you are a clever girl. I always knew you were a quiet one, but I didn't realize that you were the clever one of the family. How did you hear of the competition, do you eat this Stir-a-Brek stuff?'

'No. We tried one packet to get the entry coupon, but it was revolting, even Wolf thought so. The English teacher at school told us about it; quite a lot of people at Castleford Comprehensive sent in stories.'

'I wish I'd known: Ricky writes very amusing stories. I'm sure he would have won if he had entered. Now you must let them know your height and weight at once and tell them that you're a beginner.'

'Yes, we've done that bit,' answered Debbie, not daring to admit that they had said they had three year's riding experience, which wasn't quite true, but, as her mother had said, it wouldn't take much riding to get them all in practice again and then they would be too good for a beginner's pony, and anyway, they all knew what Mrs Jones was like, forever laughing at people on old slugs: they had to hope for something that would stand comparison with Copper.

'Tack,' said Mrs Yaxley. 'You'll be wanting a second-hand saddle and bridle.'

'No, they come with the pony,' Debbie explained. 'What we want to consult you about is the grazing. Stir-a-Brek will pay for the first year.'

'Grazing,' said Mrs Yaxley thoughtfully. 'Well now, if it's a nice sensible pony, we might take it for the summer. We've decided to stable Bucks' Fizz, we want him really fit for the shows, and that means dear old Holly is out in the field on her own. We don't want anything with ringworm, or red worm for that matter, or a pony that kicks – but if they give you a nice, sensible animal I'd be quite glad to take it as a companion for Holly. As for cost, I'll have to find out what people are charging now and give your parents a ring.'

'Oh, that would be lovely,' said Debbie gratefully.

'You could keep your tack in the saddle room, provided you clean it each time you ride; I can't stand dirty tack lying about. And I daresay Sam would show you the best rides. Ricky does most of his riding at shows nowadays and when he hacks it's generally with Melanie Jones, but Sam just drifts about aimlessly on his own. No sense of purpose, that's the trouble with so many young people today.' Mrs Yaxley's voice was loud and ringing. Debbie looked round for a way of escape. She could see Rachel and Tess both leaning over Bucks' Fizz's door and talking to Ricky; Sam, grooming Holly in the next box, was on his own.

'I'll just go and say hullo to Sam,' she told Mrs Yaxley.

Holly was losing the thick greyish hair of her winter coat and, below, large patches of shining red roan were appearing. Sam was brushing a black foreleg.

'Did the others tell you I've won a pony?' asked Debbie. 'Your mother says it can live with Holly.'

'Great,' said Sam without looking up. 'Holly's a bit lonely now that Fizz is stabled; she hangs about by the gate all day.'

The carroty hair and freckles clashed horribly with red roan, thought Debbie, but he didn't look weird whatever Rae and Tess said. 'We get the pony next Friday,' she told him, 'from a riding school at Richmond. There are going to be four ponies to chose from and Brian Bateman will help me decide.'

'Great,' said Sam, moving on to a hindleg.

'They're giving a saddle and bridle and grooming kit with the pony,' said Debbie.

'Terrific.' Sam moved to the next leg.

Debbie stood and tried to think of something else to say. Gradually the silence became unendurable and she fled to the other loose box door. Rachel and Tess were both talking at once, and Ricky had given up grooming and was laughing, his blue eyes bright. 'Hullo, Deb, I hear you're the heroine of the hour,' he teased. 'Chatted up by Brian Bateman, interviewed by the press, presented with ponies.'

'Only one,' Debbie told him. 'We'll have to share.'

'Well, I hope they give you a decent one while they're at it.'

'I'm not very particular,' Debbie answered. 'We won't be able to afford a trailer, even if we get good enough to ride in shows, so a nice friendly pony for hacking and pony club things will do.'

'I hope he's good-looking,' said Rachel. 'I can't stand ponies with huge heads.'

'I hope he's a showjumper,' said Tess. 'I don't see why we shouldn't have a trailer next year when Dad's well again. I'd love to go round the shows.'

2

Easter Parade

It was really the most terrifying way of being given a pony that one could possibly imagine, thought Debbie, looking across the evenly raked peat of the vast covered school, where she was going to ride, to the empty tip-up seats of the gallery. Men in jeans were erecting huge banners with Stir-a-Brek slogans emblazoned across them: 'Start-a-Day with Stir-a-Brek. Stir-a-Brek Sustains the Whole Day Through! Other men trailed cables, arranging microphones, fixing lighting.

It was much worse now she was here; her stomach churned at the thought of the ordeal ahead. Rachel's jodhs, which seemed to have shrunk during her mother's presentation wash, felt agonizingly tight round the waist and knees. Her legs felt weak, bloodless and boneless; she was never going to have the strength to ride.

She turned and looked at the huge, immaculate stable yard. There were at least forty loose boxes. Girl grooms bustled between them carrying buckets, grooming kits and tack.

Debbie looked at her family. In their determination not to be late, they had arrived half an hour early. No one was ready to receive them and Rachel, who liked to make late and dramatic entrances, was sulking, embarrassed by her parents' ineptitude. She still managed to look glamorous, thought Debbie enviously: tall, willowy and fashionable in her red sweater and white jeans.

Their father was tall and willowy, too. He looked nice

in his tweed jacket and dark brown trousers, though his face had grown haggard since the accident and he had to support his shattered leg with a walking stick. Their mother, small, brisk and bird-like, was wearing her best teaching skirt and jacket, specially cleaned for the occasion, and her bright brown eyes were taking everything in.

'There's posh for you,' she said, trying to talk with a Welsh accent.

Tess, who'd come in jodhs in case she was offered a ride, had gone off on a tour of the loose boxes and vanished among the other pony club types who'd suddenly invaded the yard.

Debbie sighed and sat down on the edge of a water trough. Her legs felt too weak to support her anymore. It'll be worth it in the end, she told herself. You're going to have a pony.

'Why don't we try the office?' suggested Mrs Peterson. 'Look, it's over there. *Someone* must want to know we're here, after all, Deb's the star of the occasion.'

Debbie began to follow her parents towards the office, but then Tess came running, breathless with excitement. 'He's arrived!' she shouted. 'Brian Bateman's arrived! I saw him drive into the car park in a super sports car; he looks just like he does on television. Shall I ask him for his autograph now or later?'

'Later,' Rachel told her. 'You mustn't be a pest, and do stop shouting.'

'Oh, you are dreary,' complained Tess. 'And look at Deb, she's behaving as though she was at the dentist's. If I'd won I'd be enjoying every minute of it, and you should hear the runners-up talking; they're only getting toy horses and they're all envying Deb like mad.'

Mrs Peterson brought a tall grey-haired woman over to them. 'This is Mrs Barthorpe, the owner of the stables.' She introduced them: 'My three daughters:

Rachel, Tess and Debbie, the winner.'

'Congratulations on your story, Debbie,' said Mrs Barthorpe shaking her hand. 'We've four lovely ponies for you to choose from and they'll be coming into the school in a moment. Ah, here's Mr Spicely-Thomas, the managing director. And Brian; excuse me a moment.' She bustled away.

Debbie sat down on the edge of the water trough again. The yard seemed to be full of very unhorsy-looking men in business suits. Suddenly they crowded round her, all shaking her hand and offering congratulations.

'Thank you, thank you very much,' Debbie said again and again; she couldn't think of anything else to say. Some of them made jokes or asked silly questions which left Debbie speechless. She was relieved when her mother answered for her.

Then Brian Bateman came over. 'Hullo, Debbie, glad to meet you,' he said. 'And this must be your kid sister.'

Tess was gazing at him with a rapturous expression.

'Yes, this is Tess. She'd like your autograph if you can spare the time. And that's Rachel.'

'She's the beauty and you're the brains. What a family!' said Brian Bateman, signing Tess's autograph book with a flourish.

'Now, shall we get on with choosing this pony? Miss,' he called to a girl groom, 'we're all set, can we have them in now? They are all between fourteen hands and fourteen-two,' he told Debbie as they walked to the centre of the school. 'They're all okay in traffic and they've all passed the vet. I'll ride them in turn, you try the one I've finished with, and then we'll have a chat and make up our minds.'

Debbie's stomach churned wildly. She felt very cold and hoped that she wasn't going to be sick. All the watchers were appearing in the gallery, and Debbie could see her family in the second row. She hoped she wasn't going to fall off in front of everyone.

But then the ponies came in, and Debbie forgot everything, except that one of them was to belong to her. Saddled and bridled, they were each led by a girl groom as they walked in single file round the school. They all looked lovely as, beautifully groomed and turned out, they paraded with light steps and pricked ears. Suppose I can't decide, panicked Debbie.

'The grey moves well,' said Brian Bateman. 'The chestnut's pretty, I expect you'll go for her. The bay's a real old plod and the brown is too straight in the shoulder for my liking. Well, here goes.' He took off his safari jacket and signalled to the groom who led the bay. As he mounted, the other three ponies lined up in the centre. Debbie patted them in turn. The chestnut seemed nervous, the other two were very friendly.

The bay's groom began to talk to Debbie. 'You're in luck, aren't you? Fancy winning a pony! Which do you like best? That's Barney, Brian's riding, he's a poppet, a real family pony. I'd take him if I were you. Goldie, the chestnut, is a real little gas-bag and the grey's only a five-year-old.'

Debbie watched as Brian walked, trotted, cantered and galloped Barney. Then he put him round the course of five showjumps and the bay pony jumped willingly and well, but without much to spare. You couldn't imagine yourself jumping off against Melanie Jones and Ricky at the Castleford Show, decided Debbie.

Brian rode back to her. 'Just as we thought, a real old plod,' he said. 'You're not going places on *him*. But try him for yourself. You give him a whirl while I see what the chestnut has to offer.'

Barney's groom helped shorten the stirrups and then Debbie rode off cautiously. She'd forgotten her tight jodhpurs and, miraculously, her legs seemed to have recovered their strength. It was ages since she had ridden, but Barney was so obliging and sensible that she soon felt perfectly at home and began to enjoy herself. She even tried a gallop, following Brian as he raced up and down the long sides of the school and slowed up on the short ones.

As Brian prepared to jump, she patted the bright bay neck and thought that she would love to have Barney for her own, unless any of the other ponies turned out even better.

The chestnut was tearing round, head in the air, hurling herself at the jumps. She crashed the gate with her forelegs. Brian took her back and made her take it slowly. This time she cleared it and the gallery applauded. Brian slid off. 'Too gassy by half,' he told Debbie. 'Doesn't know whether she's on her head or her heels most of the time. Terrible time-wasters, these hot little nut-cases; every time you think you've got them right they blow up again and you're back to square one. I wouldn't take her on if you paid me. A good temperament's half the battle. But try her, see if you agree with me.' He sprang on to the grey and rode away. Reluctantly, Debbie handed over Barney and mounted Goldie, who refused to stand while she shortened her stirrups. Twirling and reversing, the chestnut pony dragged her groom around the school. She was horrible to ride, carrying her head higher and higher if you tried to make contact with her mouth. At the trot and canter her stiff back jolted Debbie out of the saddle and she felt that she had no control. She pulled up and watched Brian on the grey.

He was an iron-grey gelding and he was going like a dressage horse. He trotted and cantered elegantly, with an arched neck and pricked ears. This was a fairy prince of a pony, thought Debbie, gazing in admiration. Barney was nice, she would have lots of fun with him, but she understood what Brian had meant about going places. The grey had star quality, he would compete on equal terms with Bucks' Fizz and Copper Jones.

Brian turned the grey at the first of the jumps. He gave a little buck of excitement and set off eagerly. They were obviously nothing to him; he cleared them with feet to spare.

Brian called for them to be raised. Then he circled and went round again. The grey sailed over joyfully, adding little flourishes, small bucks and frisks and head tossings, to show his pleasure in his own artistic performance.

Brian rode back to Debbie. 'This is the lad for you,' he said, patting the grey's neck. 'A really nice ride, well-schooled and with no end of a pop in him. Real potential, that's what he's got. Quite a different class from the other two. Have a go and see what you think. I'll try old Brownie.'

'What's his name?' Debbie asked the grey's groom as she mounted.

'Something or another's Easter Parade. He's a part-bred Arab with a pedigree,' answered the groom. 'We just call him Easter.'

'He's really lovely,' said Debbie.

'Yes, and only just five; his whole life is ahead of him.'

Debbie rode round. Light and silent, Easter's hoofs barely touched the peat. She'd never ridden such a marvellous pony. He was willing yet controllable, and his long smooth stride made Barney seem stumpy in comparison. She tried galloping: he stayed beautifully balanced and came back to hand the moment she asked. She patted the grey satin neck enthusiastically. Brian was right, this was the pony for her.

The brown pony was going round the jumps; he knew his job and cleared the fences efficiently, but with none of the skill and pleasure which Easter displayed.

As Brian finished jumping Debbie gathered up her courage and asked Easter's groom, 'Do you think you could put them a bit lower? I haven't jumped for ages.'

'Of course.' She called to one of the other girls and they hurried round pulling bricks off the wall, lowering the gate, the triple and the rustic rails and taking the pole from behind the brush.

'Is that better?' they called.

'Yes. Thank you,' answered Debbie, feeling unexpectedly brave. Brian came over. 'Canter a circle, start slowly, and, if he tries to get away from you, circle between the fences,' he instructed.

Debbie circled and rode at the brush. Easter cleared it by a couple of unnecessary feet, but his jump was so smooth that the enormous leap wasn't at all unseating. She tried to steady him for the gate, but he didn't pay much attention. Leave it to me, he seemed to say, *I* can jump *anything*. He took the rustic rails even faster, sailed over the wall and raced at the triple. Everyone in the gallery clapped.

'Much too fast,' Brian told Debbie. 'You let him get away. You've got to control the pace and the stride. You're the boss and you must let him know it. I don't mean using brute force, that doesn't work with well-bred ones, but you won't get anywhere in the jumping game if you leave it to the horse. You've got to sit up and ride. I'd like to send you round again, but it looks as though our time's up, the cameras are at the ready.'

Debbie realized that the Stir-a-Brek people had come down from the gallery and were arranging Mrs Spicely-Thomas under a banner. She had unnatural-looking dark red hair and wore a three-rope necklace of very large pearls and a mink coat.

'We can see you've made your choice,' said the publicity manager heartily. 'Now Debbie, apparently Mrs

Spicely-Thomas isn't too keen on ponies, so we're going to dismount you for the actual presentation and just have the pony's head in the picture.' The microphone crackled and a voice announced that the wife of Stir-a-Brek's managing director, Mrs Spicely-Thomas, would now present the first prize of a pony to Debbie Peterson. 'Give her a big hand.' Everyone clapped and cheered, Easter leaped in the air, Goldie turned and fled. Debbie found herself being pushed towards Mrs Spicely-Thomas, and they shook hands.

'Well done, Debbie,' said Mrs Spicely-Thomas, gazing at the cameras with a fixed smile. Easter's head was inserted between them, under the Stir-a-Brek banner.

'Look this way, Debbie.' 'Smile, please.' 'Could you pat the pony's neck, Debbie?' 'But go on looking this way.' 'Smile.' The photographers all instructed her at once. Debbie twisted herself into the required position, fixing a false smile on her face.

'Great,' said the photographers clicking away, 'terrific.'

It didn't seem like a real prize-giving, thought Debbie. She looked at Mrs Spicely-Thomas wondering if they could talk, but the expression above the pearls was still frozen into an artificial smile, which would be destroyed by conversation.

'Now can we have Debbie on the pony?' asked a photographer. 'And Brian, if you could stand at his head as though you were giving Debbie advice. A little further back, under the banner.'

'Look this way, smile.' The photographs went on and on. The runners-up were presented with their toy horses, everyone began to melt away. Outside cars were starting.

Brian Bateman slapped Easter's neck. 'Well, good luck, Debbie. Have a great time with the pony and I hope to see you at a show soon,' he said, and hurried away without listening to Debbie's thanks. The photographers slung their cameras over their shoulders, the men in jeans reappeared and began to dismantle the lights and the Stir-a-Brek banners. The Petersons found themselves alone. They crowded round Easter patting him.

'I *never* thought they'd give you such a perfect pony,' said Tess. 'He's lovely, much better-looking than Copper or Bucks' Fizz. Mrs Jones is going to be livid. Oh, Rae, isn't he gorgeous.'

'You looked absolutely cracking on him, love,' said Mr Peterson. 'I felt like a proud father and kept looking round for someone to tell. I wanted to say, "that is my middle daughter", but I was surrounded by wriggling hoards of runners-up all goggling at Brian Bateman.'

'Why didn't you jump the bigger jumps?' asked Rachel. 'You've jumped that high before.'

'Not for ages, and I didn't want to jag Easter's mouth or fall off in front of everyone.' answered Debbie, and then, realizing that Rachel was jealous, envious of Easter, she jumped off and offered, 'Would you like a go on him now?'

'Not in white jeans. . . .'

'I would, I would,' Tess interrupted her. But then, as Tess mounted, Mrs Barthorpe appeared.

'I'm afraid I'll have to ask you to leave the school now; we have a Ride waiting to come in,' she explained. 'Virginia,' she called the groom, 'will you take Easter back to his box? And perhaps Mr and Mrs Peterson would come along to my office and discuss transport and the type of saddle and bridle you require. I'm to have it fitted here and send it on to you with the pony.'

Mr Peterson limped beside Mrs Barthorpe; Mrs Peterson followed behind with her daughters.

'I do hope he's not *too* good for us,' she said.

'Of course not, Mum, he's absolutely perfect,' Tess told her confidently. 'We don't want some dreary beginners' pony for Melanie Jones to sneer at.'

'One of the girl grooms wanted me to have Barney, the bay,' said Debbie. 'But Brian Bateman was against it, he said Barney was an "old plod" and that I wouldn't get anywhere with him. Easter's lovely to ride and very obliging.'

'I admit that he's much the most beautiful and that you looked a picture on him, it's just that I felt we've been rushed into him; I'd have liked a proper talk with Brian Bateman.'

'There was no time for proper talks with anyone,' said Debbie. 'They just put on their toothpastey smiles and said, "Well done!" If it wasn't for Easter, it would have been a terrible waste of a morning.'

3

Too good for the Petersons

Easter came on Monday. Debbie had wanted to have him delivered direct to the Yaxleys', but she was overruled. All Tess's friends were eager to see him and she couldn't very well invite them into the Yaxleys' yard. The Lomaxes, who lived in the other half of the Petersons' semi-detached house, had a new cine camera and wanted to film the arrival. And then a reporter from the *Castleford Mercury* telephoned to say that he would be coming with a photographer to cover the event.

'An *event* on our own doorstep. Deb has put Long View Road on the map. Well, at least I'll be able to watch it on the Lomaxes' home movies,' teased Mr Peterson limping off to work via the bus stop.

'Wouldn't it be super if Melanie and Mrs Jones came by in the middle of it all,' said Tess. 'But anyway they'll see the photograph of Deb and Easter in the paper.'

'It's only the local rag,' Rachel said contemptuously. 'Masses of boring darts teams and town councillors get their photographs in the *Mercury*.'

'It's terribly boring *being* photographed,' said Debbie. 'I'm longing for the fuss to be over so that I can start the enjoyable bit. Where shall we take Easter for his first ride?'

'I'm glad you're not having your head turned by all this attention,' said Mrs Peterson, who was brushing Wolfgang's hairs off her best jacket in honour of the Press. 'Dear down-to-earth Deb,' she added, giving

Debbie a passing hug.

The horsebox was late. Tess and her friends seemed to take this as a personal affront. They couldn't wait patiently, but milled endlessly round the front garden and constantly asked Debbie what she *thought* could have happened? To escape them, Debbie went out into the road. The sun was shining and the air smelled deliciously sweet; every garden seemed to be full of blossoming trees and flowers. The whole summer lay ahead, thought Debbie joyfully. She was imagining lazy rides through sun-dappled woods when the horsebox appeared, turning cautiously round the corner from the Cutters' Green road.

Debbie waved to the driver and ran back to number seven calling that Easter had arrived. Tess and her friends poured into the road and Mr Lomax, a retired bank manager, leapt to his feet slopping coffee over his neat, grey suit. Debbie left her mother mopping him dry, and rushed out to the box which had parked at the gate. Tess was talking to the driver and all her friends were crammed into the groom's compartment giving admiring cries and pushing each other, as they struggled to stroke the grey neck.

The driver lowered the ramp, unbolted Easter's compartment, and led him down. He was even more beautiful than Debbie remembered as, head high, ears pricked, he looked about him with an excited expression.

It wasn't much of a place to have arrived at, thought Debbie, seeing Long View Road through his eyes; no field, no stable, no other ponies. She gave him a piece of bread. 'We've got a field and a friend for you,' she told him, 'and we'll take you there in just a minute.'

A damp Mr Lomax was filming the scene as Tess's friends pressed round Easter, when a car drew up and two men jumped out.

'*Castleford Mercury*,' said the one with a bushy beard.

'Which of you is Debbie Patterson?'

'Peterson,' shrieked Tess's friends, pushing Debbie forward.

'Great, now we'd like a shot of you leading the pony down the ramp.'

The horsebox driver was good-natured and did his best to persuade Easter to re-perform his arrival. But the pony had done enough travelling for one day, and refused to set foot on the ramp. With ears back and a mulish expression, he reversed down Long View Road in a series of half rears, dragging the driver after him, and ignoring Debbie's efforts to tempt him forward with bread. In the end the photographer agreed to take him standing outside the gate of number seven, with the horsebox in the background. He took several shots of Debbie alone with Easter, then dozens of the family group looking up at Easter lovingly. By the time he started on the reception committee and had arranged Tess's friends round the Petersons, swelled the group with Mrs Lomax and the horsebox driver and made Mr Lomax, whose cine camera had stuck, pretend to be filming, Easter decided that he had had enough and dragged Debbie away up the road. She dragged him back, but he refused to stand any more and scattered everyone by twirling round and round.

'I think we'd better take him to his field,' said Debbie. 'Could someone fetch the saddle and bridle?'

Mrs Peterson said she would give the reporter all the background information and took him into the house for coffee. The horsebox driver refused coffee and, putting up the ramp, drove away.

Everyone else tried to help with girthing the new and horribly stiff saddle on the reversing Easter. Rachel, being tall, was much the most useful person, but even she was doubtful about bridling him in the middle of the road.

'He's going to give a half rear and escape from us when we're holding him with headcollar round his neck,' she said. 'Then he'll be cantering up and down the road, in his saddle and we'll never catch him.'

'And Melanie Jones will chose just that moment to come out,' shrieked Tess.

'If I take off the noseband and let down the bit a couple of holes I should think he could wear it over his headcollar like a trekking pony,' decided Debbie, struggling to unbuckle the stiff straps. 'Would you like first ride?' she asked Rachel, when at last Easter was bridled.

'No, you go first; he's your pony.'

'Sure?'

'Sure. Tess, come and hold him while I leg Deb up.'

Tess left her friends, who were now gossiping about school, and took Easter's reins. Excitement seemed to be making him grow taller by the minute and to Debbie, settled in the saddle with the stirrups more or less the right length, he felt enormous. Like a sixteen hand horse, she thought, bouncing and swerving down Long View Road. He no longer seemed the same well-trained pony which had glided round the covered school so obediently; he had become a tense accumulation of pent-up energy, liable to erupt or explode at any moment.

Nervous in this strange place, and with no older pony to give him confidence, Easter eyed each garden gate suspiciously, as though expecting wild beasts to leap out at him from behind the wooden bars and wrought-iron squirls and, to keep a safe distance, he insisted on trotting down the exact middle of the road. This didn't matter on the estate where there was very little traffic, but when they turned into the Cutters' Green road, and he still resisted all Debbie's efforts to control him and shied continuously from one side of the road to the other, a stream of impatient motorists quickly built up behind them. Some began to hoot angrily, exciting Easter even more. Desperately Debbie looked for a passing place, so that she could let them by, but there was no grass verge and all the garden gates were either shut or had their driveways blocked by cars. She had to trot on until she reached the green, then, with a sigh of relief, she rode on to the grass and turned in her saddle to shout her thanks to the trapped drivers. Easter seized his opportunity: with a light-hearted buck he broke into a canter and raced away across the inviting turf. Taken by surprise, half unseated by the buck, Debbie was helpless. Her crash cap was over her eyes, her reins were too long and she'd lost a stirrup. Hurtling across the green at what felt like racehorse speed, she struggled to sort herself out. She pushed her hat back on, groped for her stirrup, shortened her reins. Then she tried to slow Easter up, but he ignored her. She pulled harder and harder on the reins, but with his head low, he pulled harder too and seemed to go even faster. He's running away, she thought. Fighting a feeling of rising panic, she tried calling, 'Whoa, Easter, whoa,' in a calm and soothing voice, but that had no effect either. They raced on, the wind in her face, the frightening feeling of out-of-control power beneath her, once round the green, twice round, with no slackening of speed.

As they started the third circuit, with Easter pulling as hard as ever, she heard voices shouting to her, 'Circle. *Circle*, Debbie. Pull him round.'

She tried tugging at one rein and he changed direction, heading across the centre of the green, straight towards the carefully mown patch that was the summer cricket pitch. She couldn't circle on that, so she let him straighten up and they thundered on. He was heading for the road now, she had to turn him away. Desperately she hauled on one rein; he resisted her. She tried again and again, knowing that if he careered on to the road at this pace he would be bound to slip and fall, even if he escaped colliding with a car. She pulled again with frantic strength and then, with immense relief, felt him begin to turn. He was slowing down, tiring at last. As they circled, she saw a group of bystanders with a pony in their midst. Easter saw the pony too, he turned towards the group, cantered right up to them, and stopped in front of the liver chestnut pony with a skid and a lurch that sent Debbie up his neck.

'Deb, are you all right?' Her mother was one of the watchers. 'Oh dear, you did give us a fright.'

'Didn't you hear us shouting at you to circle?' asked a contemptuous voice, and Debbie saw that it was Melanie Jones, blonde and pink-cheeked, who sat bare-back on the liver chestnut pony.

'It was the cricket pitch,' she explained breathlessly. 'I didn't want to spoil it.' She slid off, her knees shaking. She saw that Mrs Yaxley was there was well as Mrs Jones, Rachel and Tess, Sam and Ricky. 'I just couldn't stop him,' she told them.

'Well, you stayed on and he stopped in the end, so there's nothing to get excited about,' said Tess.

'It looks to me as though they've given you a dud, or a rogue,' announced Mrs Jones. 'But then I suppose you've got to expect trouble if you get a pony for nothing. I mean if you spend the best part of a thousand pounds on a pony, you know you've got a decent one, but the sort they give away with breakfast cereals *can't* be up to much.'

'He looks a real beauty to me,' said Mrs Yaxley patting Easter's sweaty neck. She turned to Mrs Peter-son. 'You say he's five this year and he's been stabled in London and ridden in a covered school. I'd say the feel of being out in the open and having grass beneath his hoofs was too much for him; it went to his head. And Debbie's not experienced enough for a well-bred youngster, so she couldn't stop him taking off.'

'Fancy giving a smashing five-year-old to a kid who can hardly ride,' said Melanie scornfully.

'Debbie *can* ride,' protested Tess. 'She started when she was ten.'

'Once a week at the local riding school doesn't make you a rider,' sneered Melanie.

'Even if you have your own pony and ride every day, you count as a beginner for two years,' Ricky explained to Tess.

'Well, Brian Bateman picked Easter out as suitable for Debbie,' said Mrs Peterson defensively. 'There *was* a steadier pony, but he told her she wouldn't get anywhere with it; we weren't consulted, but after all he is an expert and he was there to advise.'

'He's a top-class showjumper and he's obviously got an eye for a pony,' agreed Mrs Yaxley, 'but I doubt if he knows much about children. No one of Debbie's age ought to be given a five-year-old to cope with on their own – young ponies are so unpredictable – and he's too well-bred for a beginner. Still, it's done, so we'll just have to hope that being put out to grass will calm him down: Some of them get fat and sleepy. And whatever you do, girls, don't give him a single oat or pony nut, not one.'

Debbie looked at her sisters. 'Do either of you want to try him?'

Rachel shook her head. 'I've only got jeans on.'

'Not now. Not in front of everyone,' said Tess with a self-conscious giggle.

'I'd turn him out and let him settle down with Holly,' advised Mrs Yaxley. 'He's had a long worrying journey in a strange horsebox and now he finds himself in a strange place among strange people. Do give the poor boy a chance to collect his wits.'

'Well, I suppose all's well that ends well,' said Mrs

Peterson, walking beside Debbie as they all set off for Jasmine Cottage. 'Half of me wishes we'd played safe and had the bay pony, and the other half says that if the Petersons want to be in the same league as the Yaxleys and Joneses, they've got to take a few risks and go for an Easter.'

'I expect that once he's turned out and can gallop round the field whenever he feels like it, he'll calm down,' said Debbie without much conviction. It was rather frightening to know that you had a pony you simply couldn't stop however hard you pulled. As they came into the yard she wondered whether she should ask Mrs Yaxley's advice. Circle, they'd all shouted at her, but you couldn't circle if you were running away down a road.

'You'd better keep off the green for the next week or two,' said Mrs Yaxley as Tess took Easter's saddle. 'Either ride in the field or round the lanes. But if it's wet I don't want the field cut up, or there won't be any grass for the ponies to eat, so if it rains you must stay in the little school we made in the far corner. It's cinders, peat and shavings and it rides quite well. If you want to go round the lanes the boys will show you the way.'

'I can't, Ma, not tomorrow, anyway. You know you're taking me over to Merton,' Ricky reminded her.

'Oh, yes, of course. It's coaching for the show-jumping team, isn't it? Well, Sam will be here; you'll look after Debbie, won't you, Sam?'

Sam, blushing red through his freckles, looked down at his boots. 'All right,' he muttered.

'You don't have to,' Debbie told him hastily. 'Rachel or Tess will come and we've got two old bikes, so we can find our own way round the lanes.'

'Gallant old Sam,' teased Mrs Jones, 'always the perfect gentleman.'

'I said "all right",' Sam snapped at her.

Easter seemed delighted with his field and very pleased to have Holly as a friend. After a gallop round and a few loud mustang-like snorts, he settled down to graze, moving side by side and step by step with the roan pony.

'I must go into Castleford this afternoon and buy some saddle soap,' said Debbie as the Petersons walked slowly home. 'There's a can of hoof oil in the grooming kit, but no tack cleaning things. I don't want to upset Mrs Yaxley by leaving the tack dirty or by using her saddle soap.'

'I think it's rather tiresome having to have everything so perfect,' complained Tess. 'Not a weed in the yard nor a speck of scum on the water trough. I'd hate to be one of Mrs Yaxley's children; do you think she's as fussy about the boys' bedrooms?'

'No, I think she bothers more about the stables than the house,' answered Mrs Peterson, 'and it's marvellous for Easter. He's not the sort of pony you can turn out in any old field, he's got to have good fences and a shelter.'

'Mrs Jones didn't think much of him,' observed Rachel.

'Mrs Jones doesn't know the first thing about ponies.'

'It was just our luck that she should come along when Deb was being run away with. We'll never live *that* down,' said Rachel gloomily.

'We've *got* to get him going well. We'll have to enter him for something at the Castleford show and *prove* we're not hopeless beginners,' decided Tess.

'He might do well in the showing, because he's so good-looking, but we don't ride well enough for anything else,' said Debbie despondently.

'It's early days yet, you and Easter have got to get to know each other. And remember that Brian Bateman thought you were good enough, and he knows a lot more than Melanie.'

But he was in a hurry, thought Debbie, and he didn't pay much attention to me, or ask me any questions. He just chose the best pony, and it's going to be really awful if I'm not good enough to ride him.

'Anyway, Rae and I are going to ride him tomorrow and she's the most experienced of us and I'm the bravest so *we* should be all right,' said Tess confidently.

4

Don't tell Mum

'Now you will be careful, won't you? I can't bear any more accidents, my legs are still shaking from watching Debbie's John Gilpin act yesterday. Wear your crash caps and stick together.'

'Yes, Mum,' Tess answered briskly. 'Shall we take Wolfie?'

'Better not, we don't know what Easter's like with dogs.'

'And seeing a great hairy wolf on short dachshund legs might give him the fright of his life,' said Rachel, hugging Wolfgang.

They got the bicycles out of the garden shed. There were only two left from the family bicycling craze that had ended with Mr Peterson's accident, the two smaller bikes had been sold, but these were ancient battered models that no one else wanted. They needed oiling and squeaked and groaned and rattled as two Petersons rode and one ran.

It was another lovely spring day with sunshine and scudding clouds, and a cuckoo calling across the fields. Debbie felt hope rising in her; things would go better today, she decided, Easter would have stretched his legs, he could be calm and full of grass – too fat to run away.

As they came in sight of Jasmine Cottage they could see the Yaxley car and trailer coming slowly out of the gate. Ricky, in the passenger seat, waved enthusiastically. They waved back.

'Too late again!' announced Tess dramatically. Clutching her heart, she gave Rachel a cheeky look.

'I am *not* interested,' Rachel told her coldly. 'We all know that Melanie is his girlfriend.'

Sam had already caught and groomed Holly. He took one look at the three Petersons, turned bright red, and saying, 'You know where everything is, don't you?' he retreated into the cottage through the back door.

'Oh, he is wet,' said Rachel indignantly.

'If only Ricky was looking after us,' moaned Tess. 'He's so gorgeous, and I really do think he likes us a bit.'

They collected the grooming tools, the headcollar, saddle and bridle, for Mrs Yaxley had said they were to use the shelter as their stable.

Easter came to meet them. He looked noble, thought Debbie, walking across the field with his head high and his long, swinging stride. He searched politely in their pockets.

'Isn't he lovely,' said Tess. 'So beautiful and sweet-natured. I think he'll be okay when he gets used to us, don't you Rae?'

'I've no idea,' Rachel shrugged the question aside. 'I haven't even ridden him yet; he's Debbie's pony, ask her.'

'You're having first ride this morning,' Debbie told her indignantly, 'and I did *offer* yesterday. . . .'

'Don't start arguing,' Tess interrupted hastily, 'let's get on with the grooming. Can I have the water brush and do his mane and tail? Thanks, Deb. Karen uses the dandy brush on Magpie's tail, she says the water brush is useless, but Easter's tail is so elegant I'm going to treat it with the greatest care.'

Easter didn't think much of being groomed by three people at once. He made faces at Rachel, body-brushing his stomach, and tried to cow-kick, but this was difficult, for he had only three legs to stand on as

Debbie picked out his hoofs.

They saddled up. Rachel mounted and began to complain about the stiffness of the new stirrup leathers, which dug into her jean-clad legs. Then she rode away at a walk, towards the peat and cinder school, in the far corner of the field.

It was a nice, large, flat field, thought Debbie, following her. And very well looked after. No messy corners full of docks and nettles, no patches of long sour grass.

'Lovely jumps, nearly as good as the ones at the Southgate Equestrian Centre,' said Tess. 'Do you think we're allowed to jump them?'

'Mrs Yaxley didn't say. I should think we'd better just use the cavaletti until we've asked.'

Rachel was trotting round the school. Easter looked wonderful, his head carried proudly on an arched neck, and he moved lightly and delicately, almost dancing along the peat track.

Brian Bateman was right, thought Debbie, having a pony like Easter was a challenge, you had to work to be good enough for him, you had to turn yourself into a really competent rider.

Rachel was cantering, floating round the school. And she looked like a good rider already, far better than when she rode Karen's Magpie. With a sudden rush of jealousy, Debbie wondered whether Easter went better for Rachel than he did for her. He was *her* pony. But Dad said I looked terrific on him, she reminded herself. And anyway, it doesn't matter who's best, the point is can we manage him, can we control a five-year-old, and prove Mrs Yaxley and Melanie wrong?

Rachel rode round on both reins; she was obviously enjoying herself, and she kept patting Easter.

Tess, who could never keep still for long, was moving the cavaletti. She made a jump of two of them in the centre of the school and called to Rachel to try it.

Rachel pulled up her stirrups, turned, and came cantering quietly up the school. Suddenly Easter realized that there was a jump ahead, his expression changed, and he hurled himself at it as though it were four feet high rather than two. As he landed he bucked with pleasure and excitement. He gave three bucks, one after the other. The first had Rachel clinging round his neck, the second shot her over his shoulder. Debbie and Tess ran to her as Easter raced away, full gallop round the field.

'Are you all right?'

'I think so,' Rachel sat up and rubbed her arm. 'It hurts, but it moves, so I don't think it's broken.'

Debbie left Tess to console Rachel and ran across the field. Easter had stopped and was looking over the gate. He whinnied to Holly. He let himself be caught and Debbie inspected the tack anxiously, but the new reins were unbroken.

'You are a bad boy,' she told him. 'Surely there's no need to go mad and buck poor Rachel off just because you've jumped two foot?' He still seemed very excited, so she led him back to the school.

'Do you want another go?' she asked Rachel.

'I don't think I'll try jumping again,' said Rachel looking at Easter's wide nostrils and excited eyes, 'I'll just trot round and see if I can settle him down.' She rode carefully, keeping the pony on a tight rein. He soon began to look bored and sulky, his ears went back and he stopped striding out. He wasn't enjoying himself any more, thought Debbie.

'Perhaps we should take him round the lanes now,' she suggested.

'Yes,' Rachel pulled up. 'It's your turn, Tess,' she added, dismounting.

'Thanks,' Tess looked at Easter apprehensively. 'I hope he's not going to buck like that with me.'

'I'll lead him across the field if you like,' offered Debbie, 'and then we'll keep to the road and lanes.'

There was no sign of Sam in the yard. They collected the bicycles and then, deciding that they knew where the lanes began and could find their own way, they set off without him.

Tess didn't venture on the green. She stayed on the road and Easter proceeded in a series of stops, starts, swerves and shies as he discovered one horrifying object after another. The garden gates, the bus shelter, the rustic rubbish bin and a crate of empty milk bottles outside the post office, all seemed to fill him with terror. Tess became red in the face with the effort of controlling him and, as she turned off the road into the lane, she gave a cry of relief. 'Thank goodness! Are all young horses as silly as he is? If they are, I'm going to stick to old ones in future.'

'Mrs Yaxley said they were "unpredictable",' answered Debbie.

'He's certainly that,' said Rachel.

The land round Cutters' Green had once belonged to the owner of the castle that gave Castleford its name, but that had been centuries ago. Now most of it belonged to a big company which had put managers in the farms and planted and felled the woods for profit. But at least they didn't try to stop people riding, thought Debbie; there were no notices telling you to keep out; it seemed that you could go more or less where you pleased.

Their lane led between fields and then plunged deep into the beechwoods. It crossed a maze of other lanes. Debbie knew that some of them joined farm to farm and that others wandered down to the river, but there seemed to be no way of telling which was which and Tess seemed to be picking them at random.

'He's lovely to ride when he's being sensible,' she shouted back, 'much more springy than Magpie.'

The beech trees, tall with pewter grey trunks, rows and rows of them stretching away in every direction, had no leaves yet to shut out the light, but the lane was leading them down to a wood of dark green conifers, close-planted in orderly rows. Their branches met over the lane, turning it into a black tunnel with no light at the end. Easter saw it and stopped dead. He stood gazing with frightened eyes at the darkness and refused to take another step.

Tess kicked and scolded, Easter swung round and when she tried to pull him back, he stood, a mulish expression on his grey face, and refused to budge.

Debbie propped her bicycle against a tree. 'I'll lead him,' she offered.

'No, he's being stupid. I must make him go,' said Tess, kicking harder. Easter's ears were back, his eyes were rolling defiantly. Tess hauled him round to face the tunnel. 'Go on,' she shouted, whacking him on the shoulder with the end of the reins. Easter bucked, swung round, and set off up the lane at a gallop, making Debbie and Rachel jump for their lives. Tess was clinging round his neck. 'Whoa, whoa,' they heard her shouting as she disappeared. They picked up their bicycles and rode desperately in pursuit.

It was uphill and the lane was rough. Debbie pedalled faster and faster, ignoring her protesting legs. Round every corner she expected to come upon Tess lying injured in the lane. Poor Mummy, she thought, another accident and Tess is her baby; she'll be terribly upset. But there was no sign of pony or rider. Bend after bend failed to reveal anything but a shrieking jay or a strutting pheasant. Debbie gathered up some breath. 'Do you think they've turned off?' she called to Rachel, who was slightly ahead.

'No, I've just seen hoof-marks going this way.'

They pedalled on grimly. As they drew near to the

road Debbie began to imagine worse accidents. Supposing they had galloped out full tilt into a car or lorry? She saw Easter lying in the road, his grey coat spattered with blood; Tess, both legs broken; the ambulance. . . .

As they raced along the last and level stretch of lane, she prayed that Tess had managed to stop in time and that in a moment she would come riding back to meet them; but she didn't and they came to the road. Two of the long white skid marks that iron shoes make on tarmac showed against the blackness of the road, but there were no bodies. They bicycled feverishly towards Jasmine Cottage. In the yard, outside Holly's box, stood Easter. Tess was holding him, Sam seemed to be inspecting his legs.

'Are you all right?' called Rachel and Debbie together.

'Just about,' Tess looked pale and subdued. 'I simply couldn't stop him. I pulled for all I was worth and I tried to turn him into the woods. We nearly came down when he skidded out into the road.'

'No harm done so far as I can see,' said Sam straightening up. He looked at Debbie. 'You ought to take him back. Do you want me to come with you on Holly?'

'Oh, yes, please. If you don't mind and you're not too busy,' Debbie felt that she ought to offer him a way of escape from his kindness.

'Holly could do with some exercise; I'll tack up.'

'If you're going with him we may as well go home,' said Rachel as Sam disappeared into the saddleroom. 'My arm still hurts and my legs are never going to be the same again after that bicycle ride.'

'Okay,' Debbie agreed, taking Easter's reins.

'Perhaps you should have had the plodding pony after all,' suggested Tess gloomily. 'Do you think they'd change him now? Mum could ring up that Mrs Barthorpe.'

Debbie looked at Easter. Perfectly happy standing

near Holly, he had become the dream pony again. 'Let's give him another chance,' she answered, 'and don't tell Mum, you know how she worries since Dad's accident.'

'I shall tell her I fell off jumping, that can happen to anyone,' decided Rachel.

'I'd better say that I found him hard to stop then,' agreed Tess, unwillingly, 'and not that he bolted with me.'

'He didn't bolt, he just came galloping home and you couldn't stop him,' objected Sam, who reappeared wearing a crash cap and carrying Holly's tack. 'When horses really bolt they go into a sort of blind panic. They don't know what they're doing, they crash through fences and over cliffs. Easter just wanted to be back with Holly.'

'Oh,' Tess looked surprised, she'd never heard Sam say so much before.

'But how *do* we stop him?' asked Debbie. 'We're pulling on the reins as hard as we can.'

'Horses are stronger than people,' answered Sam, saddling Holly. 'If you just use force they win.'

'Perhaps we should get a pelham or double bridle,' suggested Rachel.

'That might work for a bit, but in the long run you'd spoil him. You're supposed to use your legs and seat to keep him balanced, because if he's balanced with his hindlegs under him, he's controllable. And you're supposed to ride young horses in snaffles and keep them calm and quiet until you've schooled them and made them controllable.'

'And how long does that take?' asked Debbie.

'About six months at his age, but he won't be really reliable until he's seven.'

Debbie sighed: two years seemed a long time. 'Meanwhile, what do we do when he takes off?' she asked.

'Well, there *are* things you can do, like pulling one rein upwards while you keep the other hand down on the neck, but they're only for emergencies. You're supposed to prevent him getting away from you in the first place by using your legs and seat.'

The Petersons looked at each other in despair. Debbie decided to consult Mrs Yaxley, she might explain things better than Sam.

'I think he needs a martingale,' said Rachel. 'We've got to do *something* to stop him.'

'Be careful,' said Tess, holding Easter for Debbie to mount. 'What he did with me may not be bolting, but it's not much fun.'

'He'll be okay with Holly,' Sam told her. 'Young horses can't bear going out alone.'

Sam seemed to be right about that, thought Debbie, as Easter followed Holly confidently along the road passing the garden gates, the crate of milk bottles and the bus shelter, without the thought of a shy.

'I think we'll take the upper lane first and come home through the forestry,' said Sam, when they had left the road and could ride side by side.

'Okay,' Debbie agreed. They rode on in silence. Debbie didn't try to think of things to say, she was too busy concentrating on Easter. She sat rather forward, keeping him on a short rein and waiting for a swerve or a buck. But now he was dawdling along, he didn't seem able to keep up with Holly's long-striding walk.

Sam looked back at her once or twice, then he said, 'If you don't mind my saying so I think you ought to ride him forward and make him use up his energy. You're holding him back, which seems all right, but if anything exciting happens he's going to explode.'

'Of course I don't mind. I mean, I know I need advice,' Debbie answered hastily. 'I've only ridden riding school ponies before and never a youngster.' She tried pressing Easter on with the calves of her legs. 'Is that better?'

'Yes, only you'll have to give him a longer rein at the walk, they can't stride out if you hold their heads in, and try using each leg in turn instead of both together as you do at the trot.'

They rode for miles through the beechwoods and then they came out on a grassy heath.

'This leads down to the tow path,' Sam explained. 'We won't canter because young horses always get unbalanced going downhill and you'd be bound to have trouble.'

He's nice, thought Debbie, and kind. Most people would just tear off and leave me to cope. I hope I'm not spoiling his ride. Below she could see the river, flowing broad and silver, woods on their side, green water meadows on the far bank. Easter had seen it too. He stopped and stared in amazement.

'Let him look,' said Sam. 'He's probably never seen a river before; tell him it's okay.'

Debbie told Easter that it was just water and wouldn't hurt him, but it was Holly who really reassured him. He prodded her neck with his nose to make sure that she had seen it, and when she remained calm, he seemed convinced that there was nothing to worry about.

They cantered some of the way along the tow path. Holly's round, roan quarters made a good barrier and Easter seemed content to stay behind her. Debbie didn't enjoy it much, she kept expecting Easter to shy away from some rustle in the undergrowth, straight into the river.

Later they turned uphill and came to the tunnel through the conifer plantation. This time, with Holly in the lead, Easter didn't seem to notice the darkness.

Debbie enjoyed the rest of the ride home; she began to think that with Sam's advice she might learn to manage Easter. When things were going well, he was certainly the best pony she had ever ridden.

'Let's walk them across the green,' said Sam. 'We want to get it out of his head that grass is for galloping. No, don't shorten your reins, you'll make him think you want to gallop, just go on walking.'

5

Riding's no fun

It had rained heavily in the night and on Wednesday morning bedraggled blossom drooped, sadly and scentlessly, in the gardens of Long View Road. Debbie and Tess bicycled slowly, talking. Rachel, who had said that both bicycles were unbearably grotty and that her legs still ached from yesterday, walked, leading Wolfgang.

'Mum keeps getting me on my own and pumping me, asking what I *really* feel about Easter,' complained Tess as the bicycles clanked their way along the road. 'I felt a bit mean hiding the fact that he'd bolted with me.'

'He didn't, you know what Sam said, you just couldn't stop.'

'It *felt* like he bolted, whatever Sam says,' argued Tess, giving a little shiver at the memory. 'I just hope it doesn't happen again.'

'There's no point in worrying Mum, she can't *do* anything,' said Debbie, 'and she's trying to think out her projects for next term. If Sam's going for a ride, I think either you or Rae had better go with him on Easter. He's a different pony when Holly's there, honestly.'

'*I'm* not going out with *Sam*,' objected Tess. 'You know I can't stand him.'

'You hardly know him, you're just going by what people at school say. Though he doesn't talk much he's nice and he told me quite a bit about riding young horses.'

'Rae,' Tess shouted, 'if Sam's going for a ride do you want to go with him on Easter? Deb says you should, she says he's great.'

'I didn't, I said . . .' Debbie was interrupted by Rachel.

'No, thanks, I'd rather have my two boring sisters and the grotty old bikes for company.'

'But if Ricky offered to go with you that would be different, wouldn't it?' teased Tess.

'Of course,' Rachel answered coldly.

But when they reached Jasmine Cottage they found the Yaxleys apparently preparing for a journey, and loading the car and trailer with everything from ready-filled haynets to folding beds.

Mrs Yaxley and Ricky were arguing over where every single item should be packed. Sam marched backwards and forwards in silence, carrying the buckets and grooming kits, the mucking-out tools and the sacks of feed that were going with them.

'It's the spring jumping show at Grantley,' Ricky stopped arguing with his mother to explain to the Petersons. 'Sam and I are both in school teams today, then he's coming home and I'm staying on for the juvenile open tomorrow and the juvenile grand prix on Friday.'

Rachel and Tess began to help him with the packing, Debbie went to the tack room for her grooming kit and found Sam putting the saddles and bridles in polythene bags.

'I didn't know you were riding in the schools' jumping too,' she said.

'Only our B team, we don't have a hope,' he answered. 'But I like Grantley, there's a permanent course with ditches and a bank and water. And even a sort of quarry. You can really get going, there's plenty of room; it's more like cross-country.'

'Sounds lovely,' said Debbie, her heart sinking at the thought of a day without any Yaxleys to ask for advice. 'Good luck.'

She took all Easter's gear, because Rachel and Tess were still helping Ricky. She could hear them laughing, talking and obviously enjoying themselves. They'd forgotten Easter; still, he was *her* pony, she reminded herself, as he came over and began to nuzzle her pockets. She groomed, saddled up and then, as there was still no sign of her sisters, she mounted and rode across to the school.

Easter seemed rather fresh, inclined to bounce and jog and shy at imaginary bogies in the hedge. She tried hard not to clutch at the reins, but to ride him forward as Sam had directed.

Please be good, please don't do anything awful today, she thought, starting off at a trot round the outside track of the school.

For a time all went well. Debbie had thought out a schooling plan and she rode purposefully, making large circles and changing the rein across the school. She was working hard, trying to use her legs and seat and keep Easter on the bit, but gradually, instead of improving, he became increasingly bored and sulky. His ears went back, his stride shortened and became uneven. Debbie, wondering desperately what she could be doing wrong, decided to see if a canter would cheer him up. She started off carefully and kept him at a very slow controlled pace. She felt quite pleased with herself when they had completed two rounds of the school without disaster and she decided to change the rein. She had just brought him back to the trot to change the leading leg when out of the nearest hedge burst a rabbit, and behind it came Wolfgang, giving tongue in a series of high-pitched yaps, as his short legs carried him in hot, but unavailing pursuit. Easter exploded: he gave an enormous buck, shooting Debbie straight out of the saddle. I'm falling off, she thought helplessly, and then hit the ground heavily.

Luckily the school was soft and Debbie jumped up quickly and started in pursuit. Easter was tearing round the field at a flat-out gallop, kicking up great sods of Mrs Yaxley's precious turf.

'Whoa, boy, whoa,' called Debbie trying to intercept him, but he just swerved and skidded and increased his pace, leaving long bald skid marks cut in the grass.

Mrs Yaxley will be furious, thought Debbie, trying to stamp down the most obvious of the torn divots as she watched Easter hurtling round and round the field at top speed, obviously enjoying himself tremendously. He would like a rider who could enjoy that, too, thought Debbie sadly, who could stick on as he whizzed and zipped and skidded round the corners.

Eventually Easter came to an abrupt halt at the field gate and neighed loudly to Holly. As Debbie walked across to catch him Rachel and Tess came running, 'Are you all right?' they called anxiously. 'What happened?'

'Wolfie chased a rabbit across the school and Easter went mad and bucked me off,' Debbie explained.

'You are naughty,' Tess had caught Easter. 'I'm sure you're not really frightened of Wolfie.'

'I think he was getting bored with schooling. We'd better take him round the lanes now; do you want first go, Rae?'

'Provided we don't go down to the tunnel of trees,' answered Rachel. 'I don't want to be galloped home.'

'We could go the way round I went with Sam, then the tunnel's on the way back and he doesn't seem to notice it.'

'Okay, I'll fall off next then,' said Rachel letting down the stirrups.

'Fizz looked terrific,' Tess told Debbie as they shut Wolfgang in the saddle room and collected their bicycles, 'and Ricky's boots are real leather and shine so that you can see your face in them; his mother cleans them. I wish we could go to Grantley. When you get Easter jumping we'll have to make up a Castleford school team and all go. Wouldn't that be really terrific?'

As they bicycled slowly through Cutters' Green, Debbie listened to Tess's chatter with only half an ear. They were ahead of Easter and, looking back, she could see that he was much less suspicious of the gates, the bus shelter and the rustic rubbish bin than he had been. Holly had managed to convince him that they were harmless. It was the schooling that she was worried about now. However hard she used her legs, he wasn't going as well as when she had first tried him. He no longer showed off his paces proudly, he sulked and behaved as though he hated every minute of their schooling, and that made her miserable too. I'll ask Sam to look at him tomorrow, she decided, and if he doesn't know what's wrong I'll ask Mrs Yaxley as soon as she comes home; there must be some reason.

There were huge puddles in the lane; they weren't particularly deep so Tess and Debbie bicycled through them, but Easter gazed at them with goggling eyes and crept carefully round the edges.

'Oh, do stop being such an idiot,' Rachel told him crossly. 'Your hoofs won't melt, you know.'

'He's only five,' Debbie excused him, 'and there probably weren't any puddles in Richmond.'

'He *must* have lived in the country as a foal,' said Rachel trying to force him through a tiny one. 'I think he's just being silly.'

'I'd offer to lead him through if your boots didn't leak,' Debbie told her.

'They're not my boots, I gave them to you ages ago;

they're yours,' snapped Rachel as she struggled with Easter.

They rode deeper and deeper into the woods, the puddles grew fewer, and Tess began to suggest that it would soon be her turn. They were in a forestry plantation and young Christmas trees, carefully fenced and wire-netted, grew in their thousands on either side. They came to a hollow and in the bottom, where the lane dipped, they found an enormous puddle; it spread across the lane from fence to fence, and there was no edge for Easter to creep round.

Tess rode through giving shrieks of horror as her bicycle wobbled dangerously. Debbie leaned her bike against a tree. 'It looks as though I'll *have* to lead him through this one,' she said.

'Let me try first,' said Rachel kicking. Easter rolled his eyes, laid back his ears and began to hump his back.

'Be careful, I think he's planning to gallop you home.' Debbie grabbed the rein. 'Let me try tempting him through, I've got some bread.'

'I can't see *him* jumping into the lake at Badminton,' said Rachel scornfully.

Debbie showed Easter a piece of bread; trying to grab it, he followed her to the brink of the puddle, then he stopped dead and his face assumed the mulish expression.

'Give him that piece, I've got some more,' said Rachel feeling in the pocket of her anorak.

'Shall I come back and shoo him?' suggested Tess, climbing the fence into the Christmas trees to avoid the puddle. With Rachel's bread Debbie tempted Easter to take one step into the water and there he stood, ignoring all her soothing words and resisting her efforts to drag him forward.

'We're here for the day,' said Rachel kicking crossly. 'Oh God, he is a stupid pony.'

'Come on, Easter, please,' Debbie pleaded.

Tess had found a long spindly branch, blown down in the storm. Without a word to anyone she came up quietly, then suddenly shouted and whacked the bough across Easter's quarters. He leapt high into the air, bucked, kicking out in the direction of the unseen enemy, and fled at full galllop. Rachel went over his shoulder, landing in the mud on the far side of the puddle. She sat up and the three sisters watched the flying grey figure disappear round a bend in the lane.

'Oh, look at my jeans,' wailed Rachel.

'It'll brush off when it's dry,' Debbie told her as she ran for the bike. She was worrying about Easter. Luckily they were miles from any road. She visualized the way ahead: the lane led downhill to the heath and then there was a hunting gate to the tow path. They would probably find him there.

Rachel was lecturing Tess on the stupidity of whacking ponies without warning. Tess was defending herself, 'Well, at least I got him through; if I hadn't whacked him we'd have been there all day. You didn't *have* to fall off, it wasn't *much* of a buck.'

Debbie left them to argue it out and bicycled in pursuit, thinking sadly that the whole thing was a disaster; instead of the lovely rides she had imagined, they seemed to spend all their time chasing Easter along muddy lanes.

It was downhill all the way, so she moved fast, and soon, seeing light through the trees, she knew that she was coming to the heath. She hoped to find Easter grazing peacefully, but, when she looked across the wide stretch of rough grass, dotted with thorn bushes and ant-hills, she could see no sign of him. Then she heard voices and, looking towards the river, she saw Easter. Moving at a slow cadence trot, his tail kinked over his back, he was giving loud dramatic snorts as he dodged three pursuing riders. One of them almost grabbed his rein, but he swerved through the thorn bushes and spurted away round the heath.

Two of the riders called to the third, 'Leave him, Felicity.' 'Come on, he'll follow us,' they shouted.

Felicity turned back and they all three came cantering up the track towards Debbie, while Easter, bucking with excitement, swooped through the thorn bushes and came racing after them.

'Oh, is he yours? 'Are you all right?' 'Did you come off?' they asked, crowding round Debbie. One was a very tall girl on a lanky bay horse, another – the one they had called Felicity – was plump and pretty and rode a dun, the third, Debbie saw to her horror, was Melanie Jones.

'Yes, he's mine, but it was my sister who came off,' Debbie explained.

'It's one of the Petersons, you know I was telling you about them, Julie,' said Melanie Jones.

'*Not* the girl who won a pony for a prize?' asked Julie.

'Yes, and that's the prize,' said Melanie as Easter approached, giving a very good imitation of a wild stallion. 'Can you imagine anyone giving a pony like that to a beginner?'

'He's gorgeous, but I must say he looks a bit of a handful,' agreed Felicity.

Melanie leaned over and grabbed Easter's rein. 'Here you are.'

'Thanks very much.' Debbie abandoned her bike and hurried to take him.

'Oh dear, you've lost a stirrup and leather,' said Felicity looking round hopelessly. 'Do you think it came off here on the heath?'

'Yes, I'd have noticed it in the lane,' answered Debbie looking dismally round the enormous heath.

'Let's have a quick look for it,' said Julie.

'Oh, we can't,' protested Melanie. 'It'll make us late for the junior committee meeting and you know how Mrs Hargreaves moans about unpunctual people.'

'Just once round,' argued Julie.

'The junior committee are supposed to be helping with the pony club hunter trial course,' Felicity explained.

'And all the horsey boys are riding in the Oratory School showjumping teams at Grantley, so the girls have got to do the work,' complained Melanie.

'Not *all* the boys, and Anne and Jean are in their school teams too; come on, we've time for a quick look.'

They set off across the heath at a trot, Spreading out, they gazed down at the long, rough grass. Easter wanted to follow them. He twirled round, trampling on Debbie's toes, and tried to drag her in pursuit. Debbie decided that she didn't dare ride him with only one stirrup.

Then Rachel and Tess appeared at the opening of the wood. Debbie led Easter to meet them and explained what had happened.

'Oh no! *Not* Melanie Jones,' wailed Rachel covering her face with her hands. 'I can't bear it; she'll tell everyone at school.'

'Felicity and Julie seem nice,' said Debbie. 'They're hunting for the stirrup. I think we'd better help.'

They spread out and began to walk down towards the river. Easter made a nuisance of himself, prancing about, shying at birds, pushing Debbie in the back at regular intervals.

Presently there was a shout. Debbie looked up to see the three riders at the entrance to the wood. 'Sorry, no luck. We must go,' they called. She shouted her thanks as they disappeared.

The three Petersons went on toiling up and down the heath. Going down wasn't too bad, but climbing up again was an effort. Easter, becoming more and more bored, began to bite as well as push; Debbie could see that they were only meant to be friendly nips, but they hurt.

'He didn't go anywhere else, did he?' asked Rachel, passing near. 'I mean, it has to be here somewhere.'

'Yes,' Debbie answered, 'here or in the lane.'

It was three-quarters of an hour before a triumphant shout from Tess told them that the stirrup was found. 'Halfway down a rabbit hole,' she said. 'Oh, my legs ache and I'm starving and we're still miles from home. Why does Easter have to be so silly?'

'Would you like to ride him?' asked Debbie, as Rachel forced the stirrup leather under the safety catch.

'No, you ride him, he's yours,' answered Tess.

'Yes, we'll go back for the bikes,' agreed Rachel. 'Do you want me to hold him while you mount?'

'He still seems a bit excited; I'll lead him down the heath. I expect he'll settle when we get to the tow path,' answered Debbie, knowing herself for a coward.

They met at the hunting gate and Rachel held Easter down for Debbie to mount, then she set off at a brisk trot. Sam had said 'Keep him going forwards, make him use up his energy' so she did her best and they tore along. Easter seemed wilder than ever. He kept springing away from the ghosts and demons which he had decided lurked in the green tangle of comfrey and nettles growing at the water's edge. He shied from them into the wild garlic on the other side of the path, and then, from the imaginary monsters in the wood, back towards the river. Debbie expected to find herself in the water at any moment. She was obeying Sam's instructions but she seemed to be losing control. She could hear Rachel and Tess shouting at her to dismount and lead him, but she doubted whether she *could* stop. There seemed to be nothing she could do but grit her teeth, take a firm hold of the mane and hope that a pony who had made so much fuss about stepping through puddles would have the sense not to fall into the river.

It was with great relief that she saw the track turning up into the woods. Now it would be uphill for most of the way, that must surely quieten him down. She looked back for her sisters, they were miles behind. She tried to persuade Easter to wait, offering him the grass under the trees, but it was dark and rank. He refused to look at it and began to hump his back threateningly when Debbie made him stand.

She shouted back to Rachel and Tess that this was the turn, then she gave Easter his head. He shot off up the track at a canter, but gradually the hill slowed him to a trot.

He shied all the way home: at the stacks of logs cut from the fir plantations, at puddles and rustles in the undergrowth, at someone's dog. Debbie, clinging to the reins, feet groping for lost irons, cap perpetually over her eyes, had a miserable ride. She had never been so pleased to see Cutters' Green, and the Yaxleys' yard seemed a haven, a port in a storm.

She unsaddled Easter and turned him out. As she stood at the gate watching him roll she had to fight hard to hold back her tears. It was so awful that it should all turn out like this, to win a really beautiful pony and then not to enjoy riding him one bit.

She let Wolfie out of the saddle room. As he skipped round her on dachshund legs, his hairy wolf-face all grins, she decided that perhaps dogs were really nicer than ponies.

When Rachel and Tess arrived she was cleaning her tack with the sort of desperate speed that can sometimes keep miserable thoughts away.

'We had to carry the bikes the whole way along the river path,' Tess told her accusingly.

'That sticky mud simply clogs the wheels up. They

wouldn't move. It's going to take ages to clean them,' complained Rachel. 'Oh, come on, leave the tack. We're going to be late for lunch as it is and Mum will be fussing.'

Mrs Peterson was stirring kedgeree. 'How did it go?' she asked brightly, 'did you have fun?'

'No,' Rachel slumped down on the pine bench. 'We had a really horrible morning. That silly pony won't go through puddles, that idiot Tess whacked him with a great branch, so he bucked me off *into* a puddle. We then spent hours looking for a lost stirrup and leather, and, finally, the bikes got bogged down on the river path and we had to carry them for miles.'

'I only whacked him because you two couldn't get him through,' Tess defended herself, 'and Mum, the worst of it was that Melanie Jones was riding on the heath and she caught Easter for us and made some more sniffy remarks.'

Mrs Peterson laughed. 'What a morning! Well, eat and you'll feel better; you'll start to see the funny side.'

'I won't, it's no use pretending that you can have fun with three people sharing one pony, and those two grotty old bikes are only fit for scrap,' said Rachel bitterly.

They did feel slightly better when they had finished the kedgeree and started on the tinned peaches, but Rachel was still firm. 'I am *not* going round the lanes on those bikes again, not for anyone,' she announced.

'But I don't like any of you riding alone, especially on a young pony,' said Mrs Peterson. 'Supposing you come off?'

'But Deb was alone, practically the whole way home,' Tess told her. 'She couldn't stop and we couldn't start.'

'Oh dear, I thought you were getting the hang of him,' Mrs Peterson looked at Debbie. 'You said he went so well yesterday.'

'That was out with Sam. He's okay with another pony.'

'Well then, perhaps fate decreed my meeting this morning. I went to the library, in search of inspiration for next term, and on the doorstep I ran into Mrs Hargreaves: she's the secretary of the pony club. She had heard all about Easter from Mrs Jones and seemed rather shocked that they should have given a five-year-old to "comparatively inexperienced riders".'

'She's politer than Melanie then,' interrupted Tess. '*She's* still telling everyone we're beginners.'

'Then she said you ought to join the pony club, she says it's well worth the subscription and they really do give you help and advice. She's going to send me all the information about family membership and she wants you to take Easter to the hunter trials on Friday. There's a special class for novice riders.'

'Don't be silly, Mum, I couldn't possibly take him to hunter trials yet,' said Debbie aghast.

'But she says the jumps really are tiny, much smaller than you jumped at the Equestrian Centre. 'It's just the thing to get a young pony going. And it's very friendly, only the pony club members, and you'll get lots of good advice. I said you'd go.'

6

I'm just not good enough

'I'm going over to Karen's today,' said Tess at breakfast on Thursday morning. 'I haven't been over for a week,' she added defensively. 'We're going to make a new course for Magpie and give her a school for the hunter trials.'

'You'll go out with Debbie and Easter, won't you, Rae?' asked Mrs Peterson.

'No, I've got a sore leg. Those stiff new stirrup leathers have rubbed a hole in me. Jeans aren't much of a protection.'

'Oh, Rae, why didn't you tell me before? You know I've been meaning to buy you some new jodhs. We'll go into Castleford this morning; then you and Debbie can ride this afternoon.'

Rachel sighed. 'It's no use pretending, Mum, I've told you that it's no fun sharing Easter. It's stupid for you to ruin yourself buying me new jodhs when I don't *want* to ride Debbie's dotty pony.'

Debbie decided that she now knew how sinking ships feel when the rats begin to leave them. The others were deserting her, leaving her to cope alone with the rebellious Easter. But I won him, she reminded herself, he's mine, not Rachel's or Tess's. She squared her shoulders. 'It's all right, I'll manage,' she told her mother. 'Sam should be home from Grantley and if he can come out with me on Holly, Easter will be quite okay; it gives him confidence to have another pony there.'

'I can understand that, he is only five, and I expect he was reared on a farm before he went to the Southgate Riding School; then suddenly he's whisked away from all the horses and people he knows to a new place and to new riders he doesn't trust; he's bound to be apprehensive. But I'm sure you'll get him going in the end, Deb; it just needs patience and perseverance.'

It's my own fault, thought Debbie, filling her pockets with stale bread from the bin. I should have explained that patience and perseverance aren't doing any good, that he's getting worse every day instead of better. And now I'm landed with these awful hunter trials, I'll have to get out of them somehow. Sam was her only hope; perhaps he would *offer* to help, she didn't think she would ever have the courage to ask him.

The bicycles were both caked with dried mud and would scarcely move, so Debbie decided to walk to Jasmine Cottage. She was pleased to see Holly's red roan head, with its little white half-moon, looking over her loose box door, but there were no human Yaxleys about. She collected her tack and grooming tools and went down to the field. Easter was obviously lonely, for as soon as he saw her he hurried over. At first he nuzzled her gently, but when she had given him his quota of bread he still wanted more, and began to pull at her pocket with his teeth.

'No,' Debbie told him, 'the rest is for afterwards and for catching you when I fall off. *No*!' she told him again as he tugged at her anorak and made threatening faces at her. Surely, if ponies really liked you, they didn't make blackmailing faces over bread, she thought sadly, as she groomed. Nothing was turning out as she had hoped, and there was still no sign of Sam.

Debbie took her time over grooming and saddling up and then, as Sam had not appeared, she decided reluctantly that she had better school. She didn't think that she would get far round the lanes on her own and, if she was going to fall off, it would be a lot safer to have Easter galloping round the field than racing home along the road.

When she had first started riding, one of the instructors at the Castleford Riding School had told her that there was a Chinese saying, 'Fear runs down the reins', and that you had to stop this happening. You had to make yourself feel brave, to convince yourself that falling off didn't matter, if you were to be any use as a rider. So, as she mounted, Debbie tried hard to conceal her nervousness. She talked to Easter and then tried humming 'Time to Part', which was Rachel's favourite pop song; she played it so often everyone in the family had learned the tune.

But as Easter bounced off across the field, all her brave intentions fled, and she couldn't stop herself shortening the reins and holding him in. As she did so, his ears went back and he began to sulk and dawdle.

Debbie could tell that he was longing to prance and gallop and buck as he would if he were riderless – she understood that it wasn't with any intention of getting her off, but just because he was young and full of the joy of being alive – but she dared not let him go. She knew that he would be out of control in a moment, that she couldn't possibly stay on; she *had* to make him go quietly.

She schooled seriously, making sure that he had the correct bend on corners and circles, changing the rein and the diagonal frequently, trying to keep him on the bit.

She had always thought that it would be wonderful to train your own pony, to feel him improving day by day, becoming more accomplished week by week. But, after twenty minutes in the Yaxley school, she realized that her pony was becoming worse and worse. She didn't know what was wrong. She was using her legs desperately, they felt ready to drop off, and yet Easter's stride was shortening, growing more and more uneven; his ears were back, his tail swished each time she gave the aids to canter. He was obviously hating every minute of the schooling and so, she realized miserably, was she.

'We'll try the cavaletti,' she told him. 'Perhaps you're bored with going round and round.' Some one had arranged three of the cavaletti about four feet apart and at the lowest height, so she turned up the centre of the school. Easter lengthened his stride and stepped over the poles carefully. Debbie patted him delightedly; here at last was something they could do properly. She rode over them several times, praising Easter extravagantly, and then as he seemed so calm and obedient, she decided to try at the trot. He immediately decided that this was jumping and took an enormous leap over all three cavaletti at once. Trying to calm him with soothing 'whoas' and 'steadies', Debbie took him round again,, but this time he was even sillier, approaching sideways and flinging himself over. She tried again and again, but he grew wilder, charging about with his head in the air and becoming less and less controllable.

Debbie attempted to go back to the walk, but Easter wouldn't, he insisted on cantering at the poles now, and crashing over or into them in the most stupid manner. Suddenly she lost her temper, 'Stop it!' she shouted at him, pulling hard on his mouth and kicking his sides angrily. Equally furious, Easter plunged forward and then bucked. Debbie felt herself flying through the air. She landed with a smack, face first in the wet, scratchy surface of the school. She sat up, spitting out a mouthful of peat and cinder, and saw Easter giving a series of huge, triumphant bucks as he cantered away across the field. She began to cry. She couldn't help it. It wasn't because she'd fallen off, scraped her nose and got all her teeth gritty with cinders, but because she was a hopeless failure. Everything she did went wrong. She was even spoiling a lovely pony like Easter; she was no good at *anything*. She could see him trotting circles by the gate, but she no longer cared if he broke his reins, she gave way to her feelings of despair and let the tears she's been holding back for days stream down her face.

Soon the very relief of crying made her feel better. I'd better catch him, she thought. And then I'd better take him to the pony club and ask for advice. She got up and was brushing the worst of the dirt from her clothes when she heard a voice calling, 'Debbie, Debbie.' She looked across to the gate and saw Sam climbing over. She grabbed her handkerchief and tried to wipe the signs of tears from her face before she answered. Then she saw that he had mounted Easter and was cantering towards her.

'Are you hurt?' he asked, looking down at her anxiously.

'No, I landed on my face, and swallowed a mouthful of the school,' Debbie answered, trying to produce a reassuring smile. 'It tastes really disgusting.'

'You look a mess. What happened this time?'

'He would be stupid and take flying leaps over the cavaletti, and when I lost my temper with him he bucked me off. But he's going worse every day; I don't know what I'm doing wrong, but I know I'm ruining him.'

'Oh,' Sam's freckled face looked worried. 'Would you like me to ride him round for a bit and see if I can sort it out?'

'Yes, *please*.'

Sam began to let down the stirrups. 'Will you lend me your crash cap, in case I get chucked off too.' He tried on her cap 'Great! Our heads are the same size.' Sam looked at her again. 'Look, it's going to take a bit of time, why don't you go and wash your face; it really is an awful mess. The back door is open and if you go through the kitchen there's a washroom on your left.'

Debbie went slowly, mostly walking backwards, so that she could watch Sam. Easter was still sulky; he was going unwillingly, ears back, tail swishing, and his stride was jerky and uneven. Sam seemed to be taking it calmly, he was just trotting round, making large circles and changing the rein. That's what I did, though Debbie, perhaps it's not my riding; perhaps it's the new saddle or something. And with a tiny hope that it *might* be something Sam could sort out, she ran across the yard and into the house.

It was all rather smart, but comfortably untidy, thought Debbie staring round the kitchen. Someone hadn't washed up their breakfast things, there was a bucket half full of bran on the table and a set of leg bandages dangling from the rail in front of the cooker. The cloakroom was overflowing with boots and macintoshes. Her face did look rather revolting, grimy except where her tears had washed clean streaks, and when the grime was off she could see that her nose was scraped and swelling; she was going to have to admit to falling off when she got home.

Debbie ran back across the yard, stopping for a moment to pat Holly who was looking over her door and obviously feeling neglected. As she climbed the field gate she could see Easter cantering round the school, and she saw at once that he had changed. His ears were pricked, his neck long and arched, as he cantered with a low, smooth stride; he was the dream pony again, she thought, running across the field.

'He's a lovely ride,' Sam was smiling as he came to a halt beside her. 'Really great, much better than Fizz. You have a go now and, if you like, I'll tell you what you're doing wrong.'

'Thanks,' Debbie took back her crash cap and

shortened the stirrups. 'He looks just like he did with Brian Bateman when you ride him,' she told Sam, 'so I know it must be my fault he's going badly.' She set off round the school working hard with hands and legs to make Easter go well, but the pony's ears went back and he became the sulky dawdler again.

'Give him a long rein and then ride him forward,' instructed Sam. 'Go on, give him a long rein, he can't walk properly unless you let him stretch his neck out. And stop niggling at him, use your legs one at a time, slowly and in time with his stride.'

Nervously, inch by inch, Debbie lengthened her reins but, just as Sam was beginning to shout encouraging remarks, a small bird flew out of the hedge and Easter gave a gigantic shy, swerving right across the school. Debbie lost both stirrups and clung round his neck.

'You're supposed to anticipate shies, or at least stop them halfway,' Sam told her, holding on to Easter while she sorted her reins and stirrups out. 'If you let him do exactly what he likes he'll get worse and worse.'

'But how can I stop him when I've practically fallen off?' demanded Debbie. 'Every time I give him his head he does something awful; that's why I ride him on a tight rein.'

'Well, try going round at the trot,' suggested Sam. 'They don't need to go with a long neck at the trot and it's the best pace to ride at when they're playing up. Go on, ride him forward, use your legs, both together every time you sit in the saddle.' Debbie did her best to obey, but as Easter bounced round the school, gradually getting more and more out of control, she felt utterly miserable. Soon he was swerving and shying and in desperation she pulled him right up and then started again at the slow tight-reined trot which enabled her to be in charge.

'He's behind the bit,' shouted Sam. 'You've no

impulsion.'

'I know,' answered Debbie, 'but if he has impulsion I can't control him, it's hopeless.' She felt near tears.

'See if a canter will settle him down,' suggested Sam. Debbie shortened her reins and let Easter move into the slowest possible canter; ears back, tail swishing, he kept changing legs.

'That's awful,' said Sam bluntly. 'You'd get nought out of ten in a dressage test. Shall I try him again?'

Debbie slid off and handed Easter over willingly. She didn't enjoy riding him, not one bit, that was the horrible truth.

Sam rode round and though the pony was playing up, bouncing, shying and even giving the occasional buck, he seemed to be enjoying himself. He just went on riding forward and then suddenly Easter settled down and began to go well, all his energy and impulsion under Sam's control.

If only I could ride him like that, thought Debbie sadly.

'Can I try him over the jumps?' asked Sam, cantering round her in an elegant circle.

'Yes, of course, Brian Bateman jumped quite high on him.'

'I'll try the brush first,' said Sam, pulling up his stirrups.

Delighted to be jumping, Easter catapulted himself through the air, clearing about five feet. Sam laughed as he circled and rode at the brush again. This time Easter jumped more sensibly so Sam let him go on over the other jumps: gate, wall, stile, combination and hogs back were all nothing to him.

'Would you mind if I tried a bit higher?' asked Sam riding back.

They raised the jumps another six inches, but they were still easy for Easter. 'He's absolutely terrific,' said

Sam, patting the pony enthusiastically. 'He feels as though he could jump the moon. You are lucky winning a really great pony like this.'

'Except that I can't ride him,' answered Debbie despondently.

'I'm sure you'll learn how to in the end, though perhaps you ought to have some proper lessons; I don't seem a very brilliant instructor,' Sam told her. Then, seeing Debbie's sad face, he asked, 'Shall we go for a hack? Holly's done nothing but jump around one course and stand in the trailer since she left home yesterday.'

'Oh yes, I'd forgotten, how did you do in the jumping?' Debbie asked as they walked back to the stables leading Easter between them.

'We had one down. It was a triple coming out of a combination,' Sam explained. 'It was a bit wide for her; she doesn't really have the scope for big courses. Still, it didn't matter, we were only the B team and the other three did even worse. All the A team went clear so they've qualified for the next round.'

'Don't you sometimes wish you had a pony like Bucks' Fizz?' asked Debbie.

'No, I don't want to part with Holly. Ma wanted me to get a jumper last year, but I'm not as keen on showjumping as Ricky, I like cross-country better. But, anyway, since it means selling Holly to help pay for the new one, it's out.'

When Holly was tacked up they set off for the lanes and Debbie found herself telling Sam all about the disasters of the previous days's ride. Somehow she didn't mind admitting the misery of it to him; she didn't feel that she had to put on a brave face.

'I don't suppose he really minds puddles, he was probably just playing you up, but you'll have to get him under control somehow,' said Sam seriously. 'The trouble about young horses is that they think of something new to be silly about practically every day as well as new ways of being silly. We had Fizz as a four-year-old, but as Ma's family are very horsey and she's schooled dozens of youngsters, we didn't have much trouble.'

'When do they become grown-up and sensible?' asked Debbie.

'Seven.'

'So, if I put up with Easter for another two years will he suddenly become okay?'

'No, at seven they become settled in their ways. If they've got a bad habit you just have to learn to live with it, but they stop thinking up new tricks the whole time.'

'Easter will have about two million bad habits by then,' said Debbie gloomily.

'Well you mustn't let him get away with things. Look at him now, he's only being silly about those gates, he's not really afraid. You ought to stop him by doing shoulder-in.'

'But I don't know how to do shoulder-in,' protested Debbie.

'Turn his head sideways, away from the thing he's shying at,' said Sam, as Easter skidded about in the middle of the road. 'Quickly, now use your legs and seat to make the rest of him go straight forward. Great. Keep pushing him forward; if he goes behind the bit he's bound to shy.'

Easter pranced down the lane with Debbie jolting about in the saddle as she tried to follow Sam's instructions to 'push him on' which were shouted from behind. She was terrified by the explosion of energy she was producing and longed to clutch at the reins, hold him back and settle down to the nice peaceful impulsionless trot.

The smaller puddles had all dried up, but when they

came to the dip Debbie saw with a sinking heart that the lake-like puddle, though smaller, still stretched right across the lane.

'Push him on,' shouted Sam from behind, 'keep him going, don't let him stop.'

Debbie did her best; flapping her legs wildly, she managed to keep Easter going right up to the puddle's edge, but there he stopped abruptly and she went on, over his shoulder, into the muddy water. By the time she was on her feet and looking down dismally at her dripping anorak and jodhs, Sam had caught Easter.

'You look a worse mess than ever. It's not your day, is it? Would you like me to try and get him through?' offered Sam.

'Yes, please, if you don't mind getting wet. This is where he had Rachel off yesterday.'

'No, I don't mind; you get on Holly, you'll find her a nice rest cure after Easter.'

'Shall I go through first?' suggested Debbie.

'No, I'm sure he *would* follow Holly, but the whole point is to make him go through on his own.'

Debbie and Holly stood to one side as Sam battled. Easter started by trying to gallop home, but Sam pulled him up in a few strides and took him back. Then the pony tried napping and threatening half rears and when Sam refused to be intimidated, he began to buck. He looked so horrible, bucking and kicking rebelliously as he fought with Sam, that Debbie began to suggest again that she and Holly led the way. She could see that Easter was being really awful and she didn't want Sam hurt, but suddenly, before Sam could answer, the pony gave way, trotted through the puddle and on down the lane, a mild expression on his face, looking as though nothing had happened.

Debbie trotted in pursuit. At first she worried lest she should spoil Holly with her bad riding, or fail to control her, but the roan pony was so easy after Easter that she soon felt quite at home and by the time they reached the heath she had stopped worrying and was enjoying herself. So when Sam said, 'Shall we walk them down the hill and then canter back up?' she agreed at once. As they started to canter Easter gave two enormous bucks, but Sam didn't move in the saddle and a moment later he was looking round to see if Holly was under control. At the top they pulled up and patted their ponies.

'Holly's gorgeous,' said Debbie, 'so well-schooled and so obliging.'

'Easter's great too and not all that difficult to control,' observed Sam. 'He doesn't get unbalanced like some young horses, it's just a matter of being ready for him when he starts playing around. Shall we canter right round the heath? You have to look out for rabbit holes, but if you follow me I know where most of them are.'

They cantered round the heath and then they galloped flat out up the hill to the wood. It was lovely, thought Debbie, to tear about, to gallop with the wind in your face and not feel afraid. She felt like dismounting and hugging Holly for making her like riding again after the misery of the last few days.

Sam was smiling and patting Easter. 'He's the fastest thing *I've* ever been on,' he said.

Debbie sighed, 'That's not much use if you're me and can't stick on the bucks,' she pointed out. 'I'm just not good enough.'

'You look quite good on Holly,' Sam told her, 'you just need more practice and experience before you can ride a young horse.'

'Whatever I need, I'm not going to get it by tomorrow,' said Debbie gloomily. 'My mother and Mrs Hargreaves have decided that I'm to take him to the hunter trials. Mum keeps saying the jumps are tiny and it's only pony club and everyone will give me advice, but she doesn't realize how awful Easter can be.'

'It's true the novice jumps are small, nothing over two foot, but it's a proper course, you go across fields and through a wood, it's a real cross-country,' said Sam looking serious as they walked the ponies homewards up the lane. 'He could do it and you could do it, but together I'm not so sure.'

'All *I'm* sure of is that it will end in disaster.'

'Shall we give you both a bit of a school round the field when we get back?' suggested Sam. 'We could spread the cavaletti round; it's not the jumping, but keeping him under control between the fences that's the problem.'

'You don't think we'll be overworking him?'

'No, five-year-olds are quite strong and I think it would be a good thing if he was a bit tired; you don't want him in a very energetic mood tomorrow.'

They rode straight to the field and took it in turns to hold the ponies and carry cavaletti, placing them at intervals round the four sides of the field.

'I should ride at the trot in between them and just let him canter on the last couple of strides,' advised Sam, 'but keep riding him forward and if you get going too fast, circle. That's better than holding him back all the time.'

But Debbie found it impossible to keep Easter trotting without using the reins to hold him back. Then, each time she came into a cavaletti, she had to give him his head and he was off; hurling himself over as though it were a four-foot fence and then whizzing away across the field.

'You're using the reins too much; you're supposed to keep him balanced with your legs,' Sam shouted at her.

'When I use my legs he goes faster,' Debbie shouted back in angry desperation.

'Well, try a canter; a jumping canter, not a sitting

down one.'

Debbie tried a canter and found herself racing round the field faster and faster. She circled again and again, but they were wild unbalanced circles and she didn't get him under control. Hot and giddy, she began to hate Easter for being so horrible. She managed to stop by turning him into the ten-foot hedge, then she started again at the slowest of possible trots. Easter was fed up, too: the moment she loosened the reins for him to jump, he threw himself over and then bucked. Debbie shot over his head and landed heavily. She lay for a moment, feeling too dreary and depressed to go on.

Sam came hurrying over. 'Debbie, are you hurt?'

'No,' she got up slowly. 'But it's hopeless, I just can't control him.'

'I'll have another go; you try Holly.' He gave her Holly's reins and went to catch Easter who was prancing round snorting.

Debbie watched Sam. Easter began by being stupid but gradually, without apparently doing very much, Sam brought him under control. And when they circled, the circles were real ones, not her wild, unbalanced swerves.

When Easter had been round several times properly, Sam came riding back and Debbie set off. Holly cantered calmly round the field jumping the little jumps with no fuss at all.

'Now do the show jumps,' shouted Sam.

Debbie jumped the brush, it was easy. She circled and jumped it again; she was in complete control. She went on over the other jumps. It was a lovely sensation flying round so smoothly. She jumped off and fed Holly the rest of her bread.

'You ride okay,' said Sam as they turned Easter loose. 'I mean you sit properly and have your legs in the right place and, as long as the pony behaves, you're fine. I suppose you just haven't developed the right sort of muscles to control a difficult pony. I mean Ricky and I have been riding since we were six, on our own ponies, and practically every day; we've learned to stick on and sit down and ride.'

'Yes, once a week for two years isn't much,' agreed Debbie. 'Though we did hire ponies once on a summer holiday and then we rode every day for a week; it was lovely.'

'I think you're good, considering everything,' said Sam. 'It's a pity Brian Bateman lumbered you with a pony like Easter.'

They cleaned their tack but as the hunter trials became more and more of a reality Debbie began to feel weighed down with apprehension and faintly sick. As she fell silent Sam grew more talkative. 'We don't have to be posh,' he told her. 'Just pony club standard – clean and workmanlike; no one plaits. And another thing, I'll be able to hack over with you, in fact I'll ride Easter and keep him in order if you like. Ricky's jumping at Grantley in the morning, but his class should be over by twelve and they're going to drop Fizz off and then come on and watch me.'

7

The Hunter Trials

'You don't need to come, Mum,' said Debbie, who had just hung her newly washed jodhs in the airing cupboard and was preparing to iron her best shirt. 'It's going to be a disaster, so the fewer people who see it the better.'

'Don't be silly, Deb, of course I'm coming. And of course I don't expect you to win anything at your first hunter trial, though I bet you Easter will be one of the best-looking ponies there.'

'That makes it worse. It doesn't matter doing badly on a useless pony, people think you're great having a go, but if you have a super pony and mess things up, everyone despises you; it's really awful.'

'But he loves jumping,' protested Mrs Peterson, and you rode him over proper show jumps in the covered school. Mrs Hargreaves says the hunter trial jumps are two feet; I don't see why you're so sure you're going to make a mess of it.'

'Jumping in the school and across country are quite different things,' Debbie snapped. 'I do wish either you or Dad were horsey; you don't begin to understand.'

'Oh, well, if you're going to be cross, if you want to swap me for Mrs Yaxley, I may as well go and watch television,' said her mother, offended.

As the evening wore on Debbie took refuge in fantasy. She told herself two stories: one was rather dull, her nose began to bleed just as they called her to start. She couldn't go, but dismounted and bled into borrowed handkerchiefs until the novice class was over. The exciting one was more or less a miracle. Easter decided to behave. They whizzed round the course in perfect harmony, clearing fence after fence. All the pony club members clapped and cheered and gazed at Easter with envy. And, as an admiring judge handed her the red rosette and Novice Cup, all the people who'd said that it was madness to give a well-bred five-year-old to the Petersons were heard eating their words.

By re-imagining the miraculous fantasy several times and inventing better and better remarks for the judge, Debbie managed to go to bed happy. She set her clock for half past six, which Sam had said would be early enough, and fell into a dreamless sleep.

Tess had arranged to help Karen groom Magpie and Rachel had reminded everyone that she hated getting up early, so in the morning Debbie bicycled down Long View Road alone. She hadn't felt like breakfast, but she'd put some biscuits and an apple in her anorak pocket and she wore a pair of Rachel's cast-off jeans over her clean jodhs.

Sam had already caught the ponies. 'I thought Fizz wouldn't mind lending his box just for this morning,' he said, 'It's more fun if we can both groom together. Shall I get you a bucket of hot water from the house?'

They started for Flanders Farm at nine. Sam, who was wearing a dark brown riding coat, his best stretch jodhs and real boots over them, looked extremely smart. He and Easter made a terrific pair, thought Debbie as they pranced along the road; they both had a top-class look about them. She felt rather dowdy in comparison, but it was lovely to be riding Holly; she felt so at home on her, and, as they left the road and set off along the grassy bridleway into unknown country, she wished that the journey could go on for ever and they never need arrive at the hunter trials.

It was a fine morning but there was a strong wind and Easter shied endlessly, pretending to be scared of the swaying hedges and tossing trees. Sam, not in the least unseated, rode on regardless. He seemed in a conversational mood and talked happily; some of his words came back to Debbie, others were blown away by the wind.

'Flanders Farm belongs to Mr Brownlow, he's the pony club DC, so we have quite a lot of rallies there, too. It's a nice course, a bit short, but fine for the Easter holidays when the ponies aren't very fit. I love cross-country; it's great being out in the open, galloping across fields with the wind in your face, just you and your pony alone with the fences. It's much better than show-jumping. I hate going slowly and all that checking back and finding your stride. I'd really like to ride in horse trials, but Joanna says that Holly's not up to the team. She would get round an easy regional, but the finals at Stoneleigh would be too big for her.'

Debbie was grateful that Sam was in a talkative mood and didn't seem to need answers, for the nearer they came to Flanders Farm, the worse she felt. Her stomach was feeling sick, the rest of her weak and strangely numb; she was never going to be able to control Easter.

Their country path brought them to a narrow road, where a sign with an arrow ready 'To the hunter trials'. Suddenly the world seemed full of riders and trailers, appearing from every direction, they converged on the farm, queuing to enter by a five-barred gate and a track that led between two great dutch barns.

'You all said it was a small affair,' protested Debbie.

'It's only for our pony club,' answered Sam, 'but we have more than a hundred members and most of them come to the hunter trials. Look, you can see the course. It starts over there by the secretary's trailer and goes uphill to the wood and then back again down the other side. You jump between the flags, red on your right, white on your left, and the small jumps are for the juniors and novices. We'd better go and enter, because you're in the first class.'

Easter's head was high and his eyes were bulging with excitement and, as they cantered across the field towards the trailer, he gave three enormous bucks. Sam, sitting them easily, only laughed, but Debbie, who knew that the first one would have had her flying over Easter's head, felt sicker than ever. It'll soon be over, she told herself, that's one thing about being in the first class; but it was poor comfort.

They dismounted and led the ponies up to the ramp of the trailer, where Mrs Hargreaves sat at a small table with cardboard boxes full of rosettes and numbers and silver challenge cups all round her.

'She wants to enter for the novice,' said Sam, suddenly shy.

'Oh, you must be Debbie Peterson. Is that the pony you won?' She looked at Easter with unconcealed admiration. 'He's super, isn't he? My goodness, what a prize!'

'Yes, he's lovely,' Debbie agreed as she handed over her entry money, 'but I'm not much good at controlling him.'

'Never mind, Joanna, that's Joanna Duncan our chief instructor, will help you. I'm so glad you're joining us.'

Mrs Hargreaves was ugly, thought Debbie, eying her critically, as Sam made his entry for the senior class. She had long teeth in a boney face and faded curly hair, but she seemed kind and she liked Easter.

The numbers were proper cross-country ones, made of plastic with the numbers – Debbie's was seventeen – printed on both front and back. Sam held the ponies while Debbie put hers over her head and tied it at the waist, then she held them for him.

'We ought to walk the course next, but we can't tie Easter up and there doesn't seem to be anyone to hold him,' said Sam looking round. 'Do you think your sisters will be coming soon?'

'Rachel, Mum and Dad all said they'd be here for the first class, but I forgot about walking the course.'

'Well, if they don't turn up in time we'll have to walk it separately,' decided Sam. 'Here, you'd better ride round on Easter. He's a bit excited so keep him moving.'

Debbie climbed up on to her prancing pony. He was gazing about him, wide-eyed with wonder, as more and more trailers bumped up the track and more and more small ponies gathered round the secretary, while their riders entered for the junior and novice classes.

Three young men were setting up the public address system, arguing about the best angle as they swivelled a huge loud-speaker round on the roof of a Land Rover. Easter refused to move; he stood like a statue, but with his eyes goggling at it. Then, without warning, they switched on the sound and, as crackling music blared across the field, Easter fled. He plunged through a group of little ponies and scattered them, bucking and kicking, as Debbie, cap over her eyes, hauled on the reins. Then he raced down the track towards the entrance gate; for the moment there were no cars or trailers to block his way. He's going to gallop me home, thought Debbie, pulling on the left rein as she tried to turn him round the side of the barn. But it was a horsebox, completely filling the gateway as it tried to ease itself round the corner, that stopped Easter. He came to an abrupt halt and Debbie dismounted hastily on to shaking legs. She decided that it would be safer to lead him back.

She was almost at the collecting ring when the loud-speaker spoke again. 'Testing, 1, 2, 3, 4,' it announced. Easter leapt backwards and tried to flee, nearly wrenching Debbie's arm from its socket. 'It's all right, it's only the announcer,' she told him, as he continued to reverse, dragging her after him. 'Easter, do stop being so silly. Look, the other ponies don't mind.' But he reversed on recklessly, ignoring the stream of cars and trailers coming up behind him.

'Can't you even *lead* him?' asked a contemptuous voice, and Melanie Jones's face appeared at the car window.

'Take him away from my car,' screamed Mrs Jones angrily as Easter's hocks came dangerously close to the wing.

'Sorry,' Debbie tugged and hauled, but Easter backed on obstinately. Mrs Hargreaves rushed out of her trailer and called, 'Joanna, can you help?' and a tall, blonde girl of about twenty-five came running. She took the reins from Debbie.

'Come on now, that's enough showing off for the moment,' she told Easter, who instantly became meek and obedient and allowed himself to be led away. 'Is he a youngster?' Joanna asked Debbie, who walked beside her red in the face and filled with shame.

She nodded, 'Just five.'

'Is it his first public appearance?'

'I think so, I've only had him a few days.'

'Would it be better if you rode him round?'

'I really ought to be walking the course,' said Debbie. 'I was hoping that one of my sisters would arrive and hold him for me.'

'I'll look after him if you're quick, but I'm the collecting steward so you'll have to be back before we start the first class.'

'Are you sure? Oh, thanks awfully.' Relieved, Debbie ran to find Sam, who had just arranged to tie Holly to a friend's trailer.

'Joanna says she'll hold Easter for me if I'm quick.'

'Oh, great. She rides in open horse trials; she's good. The pony club would collapse without her and Mrs Hargreaves. I don't think Mr Brownlow does much but lend his farm and make the speeches.'

'That's quite a lot,' said Debbie.

'Don't forget to go through the flags at the start *and* at the finish,' Sam reminded her as they made their way to the first fence. 'If you don't you're disqualified.'

Debbie thought that she didn't really mind being disqualified. All she wanted was to survive and to escape the shame of being galloped home, but the wide open spaces, the whole fields between the fences, were filling her with horror. What hope did she have of controlling Easter here, she asked herself despondently.

They inspected the first jump: a section of the thorn hedge that fenced the field had been clipped and though Sam's bit was about three feet three in height, hers was only two feet. They crossed another enormous field to a second hedge, a third field brought them to posts and rails, then a yellow arrow told them to swing left-handed and uphill. They climbed and came to a pair of stone walls, and after that tree trunks, one enormous and one tiny, led into the wood.

'So far you don't have to worry about the jumping,' said Sam. 'They're so small and straightforward Easter could do them with his eyes shut, but now they get a bit tricky.'

The wood was full of bluebells; they made blue pools and lakes under the trees and their sweet, sickly scent filled the air. Another yellow arrow showed the competitors which track to take and they came quickly to a combination built of chicken coops, with rails above. They had caught up with a group of course-walkers who were carefully pacing out the distance between the fences.

'It's the same as last year,' Sam told Debbie, after he

had joined the pacers. 'Two strides for Holly, one for Easter; you'll need to slow him up a bit through here.'

'If I can.' Debbie's legs were feeling weaker and weaker.

Number eight was built of logs, looking like the wall of a log cabin. Number nine was made of metal troughs with stout poles above; the seniors was a real water trough and quite big, the novices had a little sheep or pig trough. 'Easter will probably spook at that, if we get this far,' Debbie told Sam.

The next fence took them out of the wood. The seniors had to jump quite a large ditch with a tiger trap of poles over it, the novices a tiny shallow ditch in front of a log. Out in the field a yellow arrow pointed right-handed and downhill.

Debbie looked at the way home with horror. Easter would certainly run away here. I'll have to trot, or even walk, she thought miserably, and not care if people make scornful remarks. She looked down on the straw bales, the water jump, another hedge. 'I'll never do it,' she told Sam despairingly.

'You must take it steady,' he told her. 'It's okay to go slowly on a youngster, and the jumps are nothing.'

They were surrounded by other course-walkers on the homeward stretch. Most of them were talking and laughing with their friends and not paying much attention to the jumps; a few were studying the course seriously, planning where they would take off, whether they would jump to the right or the left. Some of the younger ones were giving cries of horror at the fences, saying that their ponies wouldn't jump ditches or couldn't bear water troughs.

The water jumps had been fashioned from a wet ditch that ran through the field. It had been made wider and shallower, damned to increase the water supply, and the jumps had been lines with plastic sheets to hold the water. The novice one was only three feet wide with a pole over the centre, the senior one was about eight feet. All the competitors seemed rather worried. They discussed their ponies' horror of black plastic sheets and tried to remember who had fallen in the year before.

'The width's nothing,' Sam told Debbie. 'They clear six foot in width automatically every time they jump three foot in height; just push him over. He'll have to slow up for the next one because it's the hunting gate; you open it, go through, and shut it behind you.'

'Mind you push this right down,' Sam went on as he tested the loop of thick wire which held the hunting gate shut. 'Charles Mottram was eliminated last year for not fastening it properly. The judge was a farmer and got very worked up about it.'

Number fourteen was a hedge into a green lane. You landed, turned right immediately and rode along the lane to the last fence, two gates side by side, that led back into the starting field.

'There's the finish, don't forget to go through it,' said Sam, pointing out the two flags.

Debbie ran towards the collecting ring to take Easter.

'He really is a champion fidget,' said Joanna. 'Up you get, and then take him round the back of the loudspeaker. John's about to call the Novice class.'

At the first crackle Easter fled, but not so far or so fast as before. 'All entries for class one, section A novice riders, section B novice ponies to the collecting ring, please,' said the announcer. 'And are all the jump judges in position? Would the mounted runners please check.'

Joanna was calling individuals through her loud hailer, and there was a sudden sense of urgency everywhere; the trials were about to begin.

Mr and Mrs Peterson appeared. 'Easter looks lovely,' said Mrs Peterson proudly. She looked round the collecting ring. 'I can't see anything to touch him.'

'Oh, don't be silly, Mummy, these are only the novices,' snapped Debbie. 'All the posh ponies are in the seniors.'

Sam appeared. 'What about a practice jump?' he suggested. Debbie looked at the queue of ponies, circling round as they waited for turns. 'I don't think I'd better, he might go mad at the sight of the others jumping.'

'Oh, I should, darling,' said Mrs Peterson.

'I *shouldn't*.'

Tess came riding up on Karen's stout piebald. 'Easter will probably gallop you home.'

'Debbie, will you go sixth?' called Joanna who was bustling about with her clipboard and loudhailer.

'Yes, okay, I may as well get it over.'

'Joanna, do I really *have* to go first?' asked a small indignant girl on a tiny grey pony.

'Well, someone has to and you're the least novice of them, Lucy,' Joanna told her. 'And you've no problems, Misty's been round so often he'd manage without a rider.'

'I think you're mean picking on me,' complained Lucy. 'There are plenty of older people.'

That was true, thought Debbie, looking round the collecting ring which seemed to be full of people with greenish faces, slumped miserably in their saddles. Most of them looked about ten or eleven, but there were quite a few who looked her age or even older, and one very tall pale girl who could be seventeen.

The starter called for number one and Lucy, still muttering, went out and stood between the flags. Debbie and Easter watched as the little grey raced across the first two fields, taking the tiny hedges in his stride. He made it look so easy, thought Debbie with a sigh.

A small fat pony called Bun, ridden by a small fat girl called Jane, was going second. As soon as Misty disappeared into the wood, Bun was sent on her way.

There were two starters and two stop watches, Debbie realized, so two ponies could go round at once, and her turn would be coming very soon. All the other riders seemed to be waking their ponies up but she was trying to keep Easter quiet; she let him talk to a young chestnut pony called Prince who had a wild mane and rolling eyes. The boy on him said that Prince was a bit of a nut, but that he had a better pony he was riding in the senior class.

Bun was being very slow. She refused each jump once, carefully inspected the far side and then popped over at the second attempt.

'In the novice we let you have three refusals at each jump,' Joanna explained to Debbie, 'and if you can't get over then, you bypass it; we like to get you all round.'

A pony called Raven had set off at a very sober pace and Prince was to follow him. Rachel appeared, 'Mum says I'm to check that your girths are tight,' she said. 'They could go up a bit.'

Debbie was watching Prince. He was going fast, but he carried his head too high and jumped with a flat back. When he came to the wood he refused three times, but there seemed to be a way round the tree trunks and the jump judge waved him on. Sandra, the tall pale girl, was at the start.

'I'm next,' said Debbie beginning to panic.

'Good luck,' said Tess. 'Karen's going eighth.'

'Keep calm,' Sam appeared and led Easter forward. 'I forgot to tell you to ride extra hard when you come to the wood, some ponies hate jumping into the dark; you saw what happened to Charles on Prince.'

'I shan't get that far.'

Sandra Green was cantering very slowly towards the first fence, as Debbie took her place at the start. A nervous-looking boy on an experienced-looking pony was waiting behind her, and his horsey mother kept giving him more and more advice.

'Now, Simon, remember to ride like a bat out of hell until you're over the stone wall, slow up for the wood and the hill and until you're over the straw bales, then ride for home with everything you've got.

Easter was fascinated by Simon's cream pony. He turned round and tried to touch noses, but Simon's mother pushed him away. Sandra Green's tall, thin bay, Lollipop, was taking his time to reach the wood; Debbie was feeling sick.

'Now, number seventeen,' said the starter. 'It's a standing start. I'll say "are you ready, go". Don't start before "go".'

Debbie nodded and patted Easter who was becoming restive. He was tired of waiting, his expression had turned mulish, his back was humping ominously.

At last Sandra Green slow-motioned into the wood and the starter, seeing that Easter was about to explode, set his watch hastily. 'Are you ready, go.' Debbie set off gently, at a trot, steering for the first fence; Easter was edging crabwise, planning to gallop back to his new friends in the collecting ring. They had almost reached the fence when he saw the flags waving in the breeze, stopped dead and stood, with head high and goggling eyes, gazing at them.

'Don't be silly, they're only flags,' Debbie told him. She could feel that he was poised for flight and she didn't dare take a hand off the reins to pat him. 'Look, it's a jump, they won't hurt you.' He wouldn't go forward. She tried turning sideways, but he would only move a couple of steps and he wouldn't take his gaze from the flags. She began to kick frantically, she couldn't stay there all day.

Then Lucy came cantering up on Misty. 'Joanna says I'm to give you a lead. Are you ready?' She raced off towards the hedge. At first Easter stood staring, then suddenly he realized that she was jumping and set off in pursuit. He leapt over the tiny jump, clearing by about three and a half feet, and then bucked with joy. Debbie's cap went over her eyes, but she had been expecting a buck and had taken a firm hold of the mane.

'Do you want a lead over the next one?' shouted Lucy as Easter caught up with Misty.

'Yes, please.'

'Let's do the senior jump then. I'm fed up with these potty ones.' Misty gathered herself for a large jump and sprang over; Easter ignored Debbie's attempts to point him at the small hedge and jumped right on Misty's tail.

'Good-bye,' shouted Lucy, waving as she wheeled away. Debbie rode on alone. Easter no longer seemed afraid of the flags. He jumped the tiny stone wall, the hill steadying him, and Debbie steered for the wood. As he drew close he began to falter. Debbie's heart sank as she remembered the dark tunnel of fir trees in the lanes. She let him slow to a trot. 'It's only a wood,' she told him. The novice tree trunk was so low he could step over it, but he stopped and refused to go forward. Debbie let him look. 'It's easy,' she told him.

There were several spectators standing at the side of the fence with the jump judge and, as Debbie turned away for a second try, they began to offer advice. 'Give him a short run.'

'Use your legs.' 'Throw your heart over.'

But Easter was wearing his mulish expression. Debbie knew it was hopeless. She flapped her legs and shouted, 'Come on, Easter,' but she didn't dare use her whip. She trotted up for her third and last try, and the spectators began making shooing noises. As Easter stopped obstinately in front of the tiny tree trunk, someone brandished a shooting stick at him; he leapt high in the air and, with Debbie clinging round his neck, charged into the wood. He knew nothing of yellow arrows and was quickly lost in a thicket of low-growing trees. Branches scraped and slapped, Debbie had no hope of getting back into the saddle, and when the denseness of the thicket brought Easter to a halt, she let go and slid to the ground, landing on her feet. She turned Easter and tried to find her way back. Nervous and in a hurry to escape from the clutching undergrowth, he wouldn't wait while she trampled a path through the brambles, but pushed her forward, treading on her heels. When they reached the track several people ran to leg her up.

'Are you okay?'

'Well done.'

'Jolly good, keep going,' they encouraged her, as they pulled twigs from the saddle and from Easter's mane. The chicken coops were next. Easter recognized them as a jump and set off at a brisk canter. Despite Debbie's efforts at control, the canter became a gallop, and he jumped them far too fast and carelessly. The judge blew her whistle to clear the track as he raced on.

'Horse coming,' shouted the spectators and threw themselves into the brambles as Easter thundered by. He flew the log cabin recklessly and hurtled on. 'Whoa,' Debbie told him, 'whoa,' but her cries were ignored. Patches of bluebells flashed by, she could see the water troughs ahead, but Easter didn't notice them until the last moment, then, catching the glint of water and metal, he tried to stop. Skidding along the damp, leafy path, he crashed into the jump; knees against the pole, he pitched forward on to his nose. Debbie shot over his head and landed on the far side. She got up quickly, for the leaves had broken her fall.

'Bad luck, dear.' The jump judge caught Easter. 'Give him a short run.'

Easter inspected the tiny trough and jumped it with

no more fuss, then, delighted with his own bravery, he gave a large buck as they cantered on. Debbie, straightened her cap and fishing for a lost stirrup, remembered that the next fence was number ten, the ditch out of the wood. I *must* get him under control now, she thought, or he'll run away down the hill, and by pulling on one rein she slowed the pace a little. All the judges seemed to be blowing their whistles and everyone had taken up the warning cry of 'Horse coming'. But Easter, fighting for his head and going far too fast, came round the bend to find Sandra Green blocking the way with Lollipop sideways across the track. Once again he slithered to a halt.

'Get out of the way, you must let the other horse pass,' the jump judge was shouting at Sandra. But Lollipop's long ungainly figure was difficult to manouevre and Sandra's pale face was pink with embarrassment as she kicked and tugged.

'It's all right, I've had thousands of faults already. You go on,' Debbie told her.

'He won't,' answered Sandra. She sounded desperate. 'He hates ditches; can you give me a lead?'

Debbie squeezed past Lollipop's head and trotted towards the ditch. Easter felt as though he was going to jump, so she took a firm hold of the mane and prepared herself for an enormous leap and probably a buck, but then he refused and stood peering suspiciously at the tiny ditch. Lollipop ran into his quarters.

Then, from behind, frantic whistle blasts and shouts of 'Horse coming' filled the air.

'Get to the side,' shouted the jump judge urgently as he heard the sound of galloping hoofs.

Round the bend came Simon on the cream pony, 'Get out of the way,' he shouted, 'I can't stop.'

Debbie had managed to get Easter into the side, but Lollipop still blocked the track. The cream pony cannoned into his quarters, but, scarcely slowing up, sailed on, over the ditch and out into the field. Inspired by such boldness, Easter shot into action, flinging himself over the ditch and racing after the cream pony which was galloping full speed down the hill towards the straw bales. Debbie concentrated on staying on; she knew that she had no hope of stopping. She watched Simon jump the straw bales at steeplechasing speed and decided that she would miss them out. She didn't trust Easter to steady his breakneck pace for the take off, and, as she had been eliminated several times already, it wouldn't matter.

As she reached level ground, Debbie began to turn Easter in a huge circle and, when he found himself going uphill and away from the collecting ring, he slowed down and became controllable. Breathless, but faintly triumphant, Debbie trotted him to the water. Simon was struggling with the hunting gate, Sandra and Lollipop were creeping cautiously down the hill. Simon managed to shut the gate at last and galloped on; Easter, seeing the cream pony ahead, jumped the tiny water almost without noticing it and shot off in pursuit. Debbie hauled desperately on the reins, for she had to stop him for the gate, but his eyes were fixed on the cream pony. He was determined to catch up with it and ignoring her efforts to stop him and her cried of 'whoa', Easter accelerated, flew over the hedge beside the hunting gate and tore on, faster and faster, towards the green lane.

Debbie was powerless; she knew they were going far too fast to make the turn, she braced herself for a jarring, slithering stop, and took a firm hold of the mane. But Easter didn't stop, he landed in the lane and took off again, throwing himself boldly at the enormous, unclipped, bullfinch of a hedge that fenced the far side. Debbie felt herself rising higher and higher, the jump seemed to go on for ever, then she was falling and that seemed to go on for ever too, but at last she thudded to earth in a field of green wheat. She sat up and watched Easter galloping across the wheat; he gave three triumphant bucks and then sailed over a five-barred gate which led into the car park.

Anxious voices were calling to her from the green lane. 'Are you all right?' 'There's no gate here, but someone's coming round.'

'Don't bother,' said Debbie getting up, 'I'm okay.' Somehow she didn't feel like crying. Everything had gone wrong, she'd made a proper mess of it, but she'd nearly got round. 'I'm all right, really,' she told the jump judge who was peering at her through the hedge. 'Nothing's broken; don't worry.' And she set off along the edge of the wheat.

Sam, leading Easter from Holly, met her at the five-barred gate. 'Easter's all right,' he said. 'Are you okay?'

'Yes, I'm getting used to falling off,' answered Debbie, climbing the gate.

'That hedge is huge. I know he went through it, but it looks about eight feet high. He must have a terrific lot of courage.'

'I don't think he could stop,' said Debbie.

'How many faults did you have?' shouted Tess as she came running to meet them.

'About a thousand I should think,' answered Debbie. 'I fell off two and a half times and was eliminated about four times.'

'They've just announced that you were eliminated for taking the wrong course,' said Rachel. 'Mum was in a fearful flap when you were going round, and now she and Dad have been caught by the district commissioner, who's giving them a terrific lecture on the dangers of letting inexperienced children ride young ponies.'

'Everyone was in a great panic when you sailed over that enormous hedge; the first-aid people were hoping for a broken arm at least, they were a bit disappointed when the jump judge signalled that you were okay,' Tess told Debbie. 'Oh good, they've started Karen at last, I must go and watch.'

'I forgot to tell you how to jump into lanes,' said Sam guiltily. 'You have to *look* the way you're going to turn on landing, then the pony knows by your weight what you're planning to do. It's always fatal if you look straight ahead.'

'I don't think it would have made any difference,' Debbie told him. 'I had no control and Easter was chasing the cream pony; he probably thought it had gone straight on.'

8

The money belongs to Debbie

'Oh, Deb, are you really all right?' asked her mother. 'You did have the most ghastly ride. I didn't realize he *could* be so awful.'

'*I* didn't realize that Deb had so much spunk in her,' said Mr Peterson, looking at her as though he was seeing her for the first time. 'You did wonderfully well, keeping your cool and getting that wretched pony round.'

'That huge hedge,' added her mother, 'I don't think my heart will ever be the same again. And when you didn't come out of the wood. . . . I was imagining all sorts of disasters.'

'They were all happening,' Debbie told her. 'I was scraped off by branches, fell off at the water trough and was nearly squashed between Sandra Green and that boy Simon.'

'Mr Brownlow doesn't think Easter's the right pony for you,' said Mrs Peterson handing round sandwiches. 'He thinks that we ought to ask the Southgate stable to change him for an older and more experienced animal.'

'He could be right,' Debbie sighed as she saw herself growing older and older and going round the novice course looking like Sandra and Lollipop.

'Let's leave it till we get home,' suggested Mr Peterson. 'Deb can't be in the right mood to take clear-headed decisions, and I'd like to talk it over with Mrs Yaxley. She's a practical lady.'

The public address was announcing that the last

competitor in the junior class was about to start and that all entries for the seniors should come to the collecting ring.

'I must go and watch Sam,' said Debbie, and abandoning the rest of her lunch, she led Easter to the collecting ring.

'I'm going third,' said Sam. 'Ma and Ricky don't seem to have turned up; with luck it means he's in the jump-off.'

Joanna came over. 'You gave us the most *spectacular* round,' she told Debbie. 'At least I hope so, we don't want any more like it. Mr Brownlow nearly had a heart attack when you jumped that hedge, no one's ever done it before.'

'I couldn't stop,' said Debbie. 'I'm afraid I'm wrecking Easter. I'm just not good enough rider for him and he knows it.'

'You did your best, you almost got him round, but if you put an inexperienced rider on an inexperienced pony it does take twice as long to get them going. If you had a pony that knew its job, you'd soon be whizzing round this little course, and if Easter had an experienced rider, well, he needs help as well as being kept in order.'

'I was going to offer to ride him in the seniors after Holly,' said Sam suddenly. 'He can do the height and Debbie's shown him the way round.'

'Good idea,' said Joanna.

'Oh, yes,' Debbie was delighted. 'Will you really, Sam? It would be lovely to see him going properly. I'll enter you.'

'You'd better go last,' said Joanna, adding Easter to her list.

Debbie led Easter to the secretary's trailer; he was used to it now and insisted on walking up the ramp and inspecting the rosettes.

'Oh, dear, you *did* have a rough ride,' said Mrs

Hargreaves. 'I'm afraid your pony's a bit of a handful and needs a more experienced rider.'

'Yes,' Debbie agreed, 'and Sam Yaxley's going to take him round the seniors for me. Can I enter him, please?'

'Sam? I hope he's the right person. He's always stuck so doggedly to Holly. Now if it were Ricky . . . but I suppose he's not back from Grantley.'

'Sam's been riding Easter,' Debbie told her, 'and they get on well together.'

The seniors were much faster than the novices; they hurtled away from the start at the gallop and vanished into the wood in a few moments. The collecting ring was full of competent-looking riders on large ponies and horses, some of them wearing their cross-country helmets and polo-necked sweaters, and Debbie wondered if she would ever look like that.

As Sam disappeared into the wood Felicity and Julie came over to her.

'Gosh, you did have a ride.'

'Fancy jumping that bullfinch.' They looked at Easter. 'He's a lovely pony and *fast*, but a bit much for you.'

'Sam's going to ride him round in the seniors,' Debbie told them.

'Sam?' said Julie. 'Well, of course he always does quite well here, he won the juniors two years running.'

'But in the seniors there's much tougher competition,' Felicity pointed out. 'There are always masses of clear rounds so, in the end, it comes down to speed.'

'That beastly gate,' moaned Julie.

Sam was out of the wood. He was riding down the hill very fast, but under control. The straw bales had three rustic poles above them, but Holly flew over; she jumped the water as though it wasn't there and pulled up for the gate. Sam was very quick, leaning right out of his saddle, to drop the loop over the post. He jumped into the lane at a very neat angle, galloped for the gates and raced through the finish. Debbie led Easter to meet him. He had jumped off and was loosening Holly's girths. He patted her enthusiastically.

'That looked terrifically fast.'

'We went clear, no problems, but I expect other people will go faster.'

'I've got your number for Easter.'

'Great, I'll take him over as soon as I've got my breath back. I'd better give him a practice jump or two.'

Debbie held Holly and watched Sam schooling. He looked a much more impressive rider on the larger, livelier pony. The practice jump was enormous and the associates, who rode in the seniors but had their own cup and rosettes, were jumping their large, stately horses over it.

Easter seemed sobered and impressed by the large jump and he took it carefully, but without effort. Sam rode him to the finish and made him inspect the flags; he seemed to have lost his terror of them.

'Melanie Jones has refused the water,' Tess's voice was jubilant. 'Karen's come fourth in the novice, but they don't give out the rosettes till the end. Is Sam really going to ride Easter round?'

'Yes, he's going last.'

Tess gave a shudder. 'He's brave. I wouldn't want to gallop down that hill.'

The collecting ring was emptying. Sam rode over to claim his place. 'No sign of Ma,' he said, 'but probably it's just as well; she might fuss about my riding Easter.'

'Shall I tighten his girths?' offered Debbie.

'All right, Sam?' asked Joanna. '*Don't* treat the lane as though it was a National fence; my nerves couldn't take it a second time.'

'I'll trot at it,' promised Sam.

Debbie stood with Joanna and Tess at the collecting ring entrance, watching as Easter flew the first hedge.

'He knows his way round now,' said Joanna. 'You can see he's full of confidence; he's not setting off into the unknown.'

'And he likes the bigger jumps,' added Debbie. 'I *do* hope he doesn't refuse the one into the wood,' She began to will Sam and Easter to jump a clear round.

They slowed up for the wood and then, just as Debbie's heart was beginning to sink, Easter responded to Sam's legs and made a large but careful jump. Debbie visualized the track, the chicken coops and water troughs; he might stop there. But, long before they expected him, Easter's grey figure came bounding out over the ditch and tiger trap and he began to gallop down the hill. Sam was working hard to keep him balanced, they could see that. 'Sit down, half halt, put his hindlegs under him,' muttered Joanna, obviously wishing that she was there and allowed to shout advice.

Easter did his best to get away, to escape from between Sam's hand and legs, but he didn't succeed and suddenly he gave in and came down to the straw bales looking like a well-schooled horse, on the bit with his hindlegs under him. He cleared the bales easily and then raced on to clear the water.

Sam was taking no chances at the gate; he brought Easter back to a trot and approached it from the side so that he couldn't mistake it for a jump.

'I ought to have practised gates,' said Debbie guiltily as Easter, uncertain of what was wanted, muddled his way through.

'Now, dare we look?' asked Joanna as Easter cantered towards the lane. Sam took the hedge very slowly and at a slight angle, gazing very hard in the direction of the gates; he only let Easter pop over, then he galloped down the lane for the last fence and the finish.

'Good old Sam, that was brilliant,' said Joanna as Debbie and Tess ran to meet him.

Sam had dismounted and loosened Easter's girths. They all three patted the pony and rewarded him with pieces of bread. He accepted their congratulations airily. Debbie had a feeling that he saw himself as a champion and felt that admiration was his right.

Mrs Yaxley came hurrying over. 'Good heavens, Sam, the things you get up to the moment my back's turned. We missed you on Holly, but everyone says that was a jolly good round too.'

'Yes, she was great. I didn't have to slow up at the straw bales at the lane on her and she was quick at the gate. But of course Easter's much faster, his stride really covers the ground.'

'You didn't have any trouble in the wood?' asked Debbie.

'No, he was a bit *over*-confident. He seemed to be saying "Come on, come on, I can do it. I know the way".'

'Look, Debbie, why don't we take them in the pairs? You can ride Holly.'

'But I'm sure to do something awful and let you down,' said Debbie, aghast at the idea.

'Don't be stupid. You only have to jump the little fences, and every senior pairs with a junior or a novice. We won't win, but I'd love to go round again.'

'Will Debbie be safe on Holly?' asked Mrs Yaxley, not sure how to take this new confident Sam.

'Yes. She's jumped her at home. Will you enter us, Ma – we'd better have a practice.'

Debbie mounted Holly and pulled up the stirrups.

'We ride knee to knee,' said Sam, 'trying to keep our knees level; don't bother about the ponies' heads. Your jumps will be at the junior height, which isn't quite as pathetic as the novice.' He looked round the course,

'We try to jump them all as a pair except for the hedge into the lane. I'd better go first there, and you'd better do the gate. Holly's brilliant at them, she even helps with her nose.'

Mrs Yaxley re-appeared. 'Debbie's to wear seventeen and you're to wear fifty-eight,' she told Sam. 'Did you really jump the hedge out of the lane?' she asked Debbie.

'No,' Debbie laughed, 'Easter jumped it, I fell off.'

'Come on,' said Sam, 'the practice jump is free.'

Easter jumped faster than Holly and his long stride meant that he took off and landed further away, but after three tries Debbie found that she had to hurry Holly into taking two strides to Easter's one, and that it was no good holding her back and being cautious.

Tess had rushed to tell the Peterson parents that Debbie had entered for the pairs and the news brought them hurrying across the field.

'Are you really safe on that pony?' asked Mr Peterson anxiously.

'Do you think you should, Deb? I can't bear to see you come down that hill at a hundred miles an hour again,' her mother pleaded.

'I'll be all right on Holly; she's much easier to control.' Debbie spoke with far more certainty than she felt.

'Ma's waving, I think we're wanted in the collecting ring,' said Sam.

They cantered across keeping knee to knee. The ponies seemed to have got the idea and were co-operating. The whole field was full of pairs practising, most of them shrieking at each other to wait or hurry, some giggling helplessly, a few looking highly efficient and as though they had been practising for weeks.

'You're next but one,' Joanna told them. 'After the pair who've just gone to the start.'

Debbie was feeling sick. 'I know I'm going to ruin

everything,' she moaned.

'It doesn't matter, it's just for fun,' Sam told her patiently. 'I'll wait for you if you fall off.'

The pair ahead of them was Melanie Jones and Lucy Weston. They set off at a good gallop and kept together well, considering the difference in the height of their ponies.

'One thing, we won't find *them* holding us up in the wood,' said Sam, 'but you lose a point every time you're a length apart. Get Holly on her toes,' he added as they came under starter's orders, 'I think Easter's going to start fast.'

They started fast and together. Easter forged ahead as they came into the first fence, but Holly raced to catch up. Debbie was so intent on keeping level that she hardly noticed the jumps until they came to the turn towards the wood and both slowed down. They jumped the tree trunks carefully and then gained speed along the woodland track. At the chicken coops Debbie was left slightly behind, but over the log cabin and the water troughs they kept beautifully together. Debbie was beginning to enjoy herself: the speed, the thrill of sailing over the jumps, the wind in her face, it was lovely she thought as they jumped out of the wood and steadied for the hill. Sitting down and using your legs worked on Holly, and the two ponies cantered side by side towards the straw bales. They jumped them well, and the junior water was nothing to Holly. Debbie was worrying over the gate.

Tail to the hinges, she flung it wide, and waited for Sam to go through. She was feeling flustered and her hand was shaking as she tried to bang it shut, but Holly kept her head, got behind it and helped to push it shut. Ram the loop down hard, Debbie told herself.

'Ready?' called Sam, turning Easter and, taking the lead, he rode slowly and carefully at the hedge into the lane. Easter understood now and jumped it confidently; Debbie, looking firmly in the right direction, joined him and side by side they galloped for the gates and the finish.

Mrs Yaxley was waiting for them with a scoop of pony nuts, and she fed handfuls to the excited ponies.

'Well done both of you,' she said. 'You rode her beautifully, Debbie.'

'It was lovely, I really enjoyed it,' answered Debbie dismounting. 'She's so good and easy to manage.'

'Fantastic,' shouted Tess as she came running. 'I never thought you'd keep together like that. And you were fast. Did you have any refusals or knockdowns in the wood?'

'No,' Debbie and Sam answered both at once. Then they saw Mr Peterson limping towards them and they led the ponies over to meet him. Rachel and Ricky appeared too and everyone began to pat and praise the ponies.

Mrs Yaxley couldn't take her eyes off Easter. 'He's exactly the sort of pony I want for you,' she told Sam. 'A beautiful mover, with a great jump in him and as bold as they come. Didn't riding him make you feel that it *was* time you moved on?'

'He's great, but I don't want to sell Holly,' said Sam obstinately.

Then Joanna, who had just sent the last two pairs to the start, came over. 'One thing is obvious to me,' she said, 'Those two own the wrong ponies.'

'That's just what I've been telling Sam,' Mrs Yaxley agreed, 'but he won't listen.'

'Perhaps we could do a swop,' suggested Mr Peterson.

'Or a loan. I can't bear the thought of Debbie on Easter now I've seen what he's like,' said Mrs Peterson.

'You should think about it,' Joanna told Sam quietly. 'With a pony like him you could probably make the interbranch team this year, and certainly next year. And I agree with you,' she said to Mrs Peterson, 'Easter's too young for Debbie to cope with; she needs a school mistress pony like Holly for the next couple of years.'

'I wouldn't mind if *Debbie* had Holly,' muttered Sam, 'but I'm not going to sell her to anyone else.'

Mrs Yaxley's face lit up. 'And what do *you* think about it?' she asked Debbie.

'Oh, I'd love to have Holly. I can see that Easter's too good for me and I know I'm wrecking him.'

'It sounds as though we've got a deal then,' said Mr Peterson.

'But we can't possibly do a straight swop,' Mrs Yaxley sounded shocked at such a stupid idea. 'Holly's a nice, sensible, reliable nine-year-old. She'll win you prizes at the pony club and at small local shows, but Easter's got real class; he'll win in top company next year. He's worth much more, you could buy three ordinary ponies for the price you'd get for him.'

'*Three* ponies?' Tess's eyes widened. 'Mum, Dad, we can have three ponies – one each.'

'We couldn't afford to keep them,' said Debbie.

Mr and Mrs Peterson looked at each other. 'That may not be true. We heard something today which could change things.' Mr Peterson chose his words with care. 'You all know about this big company which owns a lot of the farms and woods round Cutters' Green? Well, they've offered me the job of accountant. It's full time and not particularly well paid, but one of the perks is a farm cottage with a paddock. Your mother and I have arranged to go and see it tomorrow.'

'That's all right then,' said Tess.

'But if Easter's sold, the money belongs to Deb,' Rachel pointed out. 'She won the prize.'

'Yes, I suppose it does,' agreed Debbie, 'but it would

be much more fun if it was shared out and we could all ride.' *Much, much* more fun, she thought. She hated it when Rachel was jealous of her and she didn't want to be best, or the one who had the most; she just wanted to be equal.

Joanna and Mrs Yaxley were already discussing which pony club ponies were about to be out-grown and might suit Rachel and Tess. Mrs Peterson handed round the last of the sandwiches.

'Oh, Deb, you did start something when you wrote that story,' she said giving Debbie a hug, 'but I have a feeling that our luck's changed and that things may work out.'

The hunter trials were over. The jump judges had left their positions and carrying their red and white flags were making for the secretary's trailer. Hoofs thudded on ramps as ponies were boxed, and the competitors who had hacked over collected their headcollars, rucksacks and anoraks and prepared to start home.

The public address gave a tired crackle and announced that the challenge cups and rosettes were about to be presented by Mrs Brownlow and that the results of all the classes, except the pairs, were now on the notice board.

'We've just looked,' said Ricky. 'Sam's second and fourth. Amanda Graham beat Holly by two seconds. He could have won easily on Easter if he hadn't been so slow jumping into the lane.'

Debbie giggled and Sam said, 'If you'd got here earlier you'd know why. By the way, how did you do at Grantley?'

'Fifth,' answered Ricky. 'Two clears but I wasn't fast enough in the jump-off.'

'I'll take both ponies home in the trailer,' Mrs Yaxley told the Petersons, 'and we can settle the business side of it tomorrow. There's the tack to sort out too; yours is brand new.'

The public address crackled. 'We now have the results of the pairs,' it announced. 'First: Celia and Charles Mottram. Second: Jenifer Tuke and Zara Graham. Third: Sam Yaxley and Debbie Peterson. Fourth: Melanie Jones and Lucy Weston.'

Tess went quite mad. Leaping up and down with excitement she shrieked, 'Easter's won two rosettes and Debbie's beaten Melanie Jones.'

'Shush.' 'Shut up,' the whole family turned on her.

'But it's so terrific. Melanie can't despise us any more and we're going to have a pony each. I must find Karen and tell her what's happened.'

Everyone gathered round the secretary's trailer, leaving a half circle of space for Mrs Brownlow and the prize winners. Debbie watched Sam collect his rosettes for the senior class and then she joined him for the pairs. She felt dazed by her unexpected success, but inside a warm glow of happiness filled her. Holly is mine, she thought, and it was all so perfect because Easter didn't have to go back; he didn't have to be sold or sent away.

Sam was looking critically at the yellow rosettes. '*Next* year we'll practise beforehand and try and win, that is if you go on riding with me when your sisters have ponies.'

'Of course I shall. I'm going to need a lot of advice on how to ride Holly and I expect Tess will spend most of her time with Karen Harris.'

'And it wouldn't surprise me if Ricky started riding with your sister Rachel,' said Sam. 'I think he's about to chuck Melanie Jones; I know the signs. We'll have to nag Ma and Joanna into finding those other two ponies quickly or I can see there will be a queue of Petersons all wanting to ride Holly.'

Mr Brownlow was making a speech, thanking Mrs Hargreaves, Joanna, John the starter, all the jump judges and the many other helpers who had worked to make the hunter trials run smoothly. Everyone clapped enthusiastically. Then one of the fathers thanked Mr Brownlow for holding the trials on his farm and it was all over. Shouting that they would see each other on Wednesday, the pony club members hurried to their trailers or mounted their ponies and started for home.

Mrs Hargreaves waylaid Debbie. 'Just one thing,' she said. 'Your crash cap, Debbie. It's useless, in fact, it's worse than useless, when it's always over your eyes. You *must* do something about it before Wednesday – buy a chin strap or sew on an elastic or get a cap that fits. You don't mind my telling you, do you? Several jump judges mentioned it and we do want it to be some use if you fall on your head.'

'I'll consult with Mum. We could sew on an elastic anyway,' answered Debbie, 'but what's happening on Wednesday?'

'A rally at Greendene, I've given your mother a fixture card,' said Mrs Hargreaves, bustling away to deal with a prize winner who wanted advice on engraving her cup.

'I'm afraid she's a bit bossy, but she means well,' said Sam.

'I don't mind,' Debbie told him. 'At least the pony club people seem to care. At my posh prize-giving, when they gave me Easter, everyone smiled toothpaste smiles and said polite things, but they didn't care a bit, you could tell.'

'I'm rather glad that Brian Bateman wasn't *too* bothered,' said Sam, 'since he seems to have settled this business of my next pony.'

'Yes, I'm glad too. If he had chosen sensibly there'd just be Barney, but somehow Easter is turning into four ponies; he's been a very magical prize.'

THE NO-GOOD PONY

Josephine Pullein-Thompson

It was never going to work. The Brodie children disliked the Dalton children at first sight. The Daltons were smooth and elegant, their ponies well schooled and their tack immaculate. The Brodies always looked a mess, their tack was falling apart and they did not even have a pony each.

But now that Mr Dalton had married Mrs Brodie, the children were all going to live together. The holidays would be ruined, and even riding would not be fun any longer with the Daltons about . . .

THE PONY SEEKERS

Diana Pullein-Thompson

Lynne and David Fletcher saw a terrible summer looming ahead, a summer in which there would be no riding because their parents could no longer afford to keep ponies for them. But the day is saved when their elder sister, the famous ex-show jumper, Briony Fletcher, decides to enlist their help to set up The Pony Seekers, an agency to supply clients with ponies ideally suited to their needs.

All goes well with the first few ponies, but then things begin to go wrong, and Lynne and David realize they must do something desperate if Briony's enterprise is not to be doomed to failure . . .

Diana Pullein-Thompson is one of the three famous Pullein-Thompson sisters who are among the most successful writers of pony stories in Britain.

95p